healthy
dairy-free
eating

Mini C with

Tanya Haffner RD RNutr

healthy
dairy-free
eating

Photography by Martin Brigdale

Kyle Books

contents

This edition published in 2009 by Kyle Books
An imprint of Kyle Cathie Limited
www.kylecathie.com

Distributed by National Book Network
4501 Forbes Blvd., Suite 200, Lanham,
MD20706

10 9 8 7 6 5 4 3 2 1

ISBN 978-1-906868-13-0

Editor: Jennifer Wheatley
Series editor: Muna Reyal
Designer: Carl Hodson
Photographer: Martin Brigdale
Home economist: Mini C
Styling: Helen Trent
Copy editor: Ruth Baldwin
Editorial assistant: Vicki Murrell
Americanizer: Delora Jones
Recipe analysis: Dr Wendy Doyle
Production: Sha Huxtable and Alice Holloway

Library of Congress Control Number: 2009934238

Color reproduction by Colourscan
Printed and bound in Singapore by Star Standard

important note

This book is meant to be used as a general reference and recipe book. While the authors
believe that the information and recipes it contains are beneficial to health, the book is in no
way intended to replace medical advice. You should consult your doctor about specific
medical issues.

foreword by Jeffrey D. Roberts

If you grew up in the 1960's or 70's it was not uncommon for some well-meaning parent, spouse or friend to offer you a cup of milk to soothe an upset tummy. It was thought that milk coated the stomach and offered some protection against abdominal pain, gas, bloating and perhaps diarrhea. That is if it wasn't the milk itself contributing to the abdominal pain, gas, bloating and diarrhea!

There is a surprisingly high correlation between those suffering from Irritable Bowel Syndrome (IBS) and lactose intolerance. It is a challenge for an IBS sufferer to know whether the common symptoms of IBS, namely abdominal pain with diarrhea, constipation or a mixture of both, are caused by diet or by an underlying chronic digestive illness such as IBS. IBS is always diagnosed by a physician who is seasoned in reviewing a patient's medical history. They look for red flag symptoms such as weight loss or diarrhea that awakens a patient from sleep or contains blood or fever or a family history of other gastrointestinal diseases such as Inflammatory Bowel Disease (IBD) or Celiac Disease in order to rule out these more serious causes for your symptoms. Failing that, they can consider looking for a dietary related cause such as lactose intolerance. In some cases, simply limiting the amount of foods containing lactose miraculously cures a patient of their IBS-like symptoms. There are individuals though, who suffer from both IBS and lactose intolerance. Thus, this book truly complements diet choices for a large group of IBS sufferers.

The IBS Self Help and Support Group has offered dependable irritable bowel syndrome support, education and treatment for sufferers, family and friends since 1987. We are a community that helps provide accurate characteristics for diagnosis of IBS symptoms and treatment, forums and blogs to talk and learn about IBS. Our aim is to help sufferers generate questions that they may discuss with their own health care professionals rather than to diagnose themselves. Lactose intolerance, though, is one of the rare conditions than can be controlled and easily diagnosed by a patient. A resource such as this book can dramatically teach you how to change your diet to control your symptoms!

We are delighted to be part of this great, well-written and illustrated book that provides many rewarding choices for someone with a digestive condition. The easy to follow recipes and resources are destined to be a wonderful lifestyle guide for yourself or someone you know who has to manage a dairy restricted diet.

Enjoy this wonderful book!

Jeffrey D. Roberts, MSEd, BSc
President & Founder
IBS Association/ IBS Self Help and Support Group
www.ibsgroup.org

why go dairy-free?

Nowadays, more and more people are turning to a dairy-free diet. But why, and what does dairy-free actually mean? Just a few years ago, if someone said they were choosing dairy-free, it would generally imply that their dietary intake was completely free from all dairy foods. They might have made this choice because of an intolerance to cow's milk, or for religious reasons, or for moral reasons such as being a vegan. However, today many more people are including dairy-free options in their diet and reducing their dairy intake for health and taste benefits, rather than avoiding dairy altogether for any other reason.

Health benefits?

One of the most popular and nutritionally sound alternatives to dairy is soy. Soy foods have received unprecedented attention in the press in the last couple of years largely because of their health benefits but also because of their vastly improved taste. This has undoubtedly fueled the heightened interest in dairy-free. In countries where soy foods are eaten regularly, there appears to be less risk of developing diseases such as heart disease and cancer, and in women certain symptoms of the menopause are reduced. Much research is currently being conducted into this.

Another reason why people are reducing their dairy intake is its naturally occurring high saturated-fat content. A diet high in saturated fat increases the risk of raised blood cholesterol and heart disease— and many of us eat far more of this fat than we need. Numerous health campaigns have focused on the importance of watching our intake of saturated fat, the richest sources of which are meat and dairy produce. Now, instead of always opting for lower-fat meat and dairy products, people are seeking new tastes and more variety, regularly substituting dairy and meat with low-saturated-fat alternatives such as soy.

Cow's-milk protein-allergy, lactose intolerance, and dairy reaction—what's the difference?
It can all seem confusing at times, but there are distinct differences between these three types of milk intolerance, each showing different symptoms and requiring a different method of diagnosis. They are summarized in the diagram below.

The most recently talked about intolerance has become known as "dairy reaction." This is different from the commonly recognized lactose intolerance and cow's-milk protein-allergy, and is championed by some alternative practitioners who believe that symptoms of conditions such as arthritis, headaches, general fatigue, irritable bowel syndrome

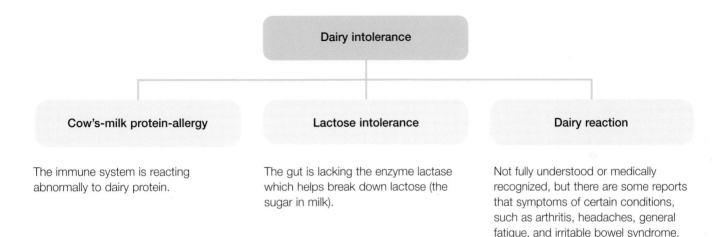

Dairy intolerance

Cow's-milk protein-allergy

The immune system is reacting abnormally to dairy protein.

Lactose intolerance

The gut is lacking the enzyme lactase which helps break down lactose (the sugar in milk).

Dairy reaction

Not fully understood or medically recognized, but there are some reports that symptoms of certain conditions, such as arthritis, headaches, general fatigue, and irritable bowel syndrome, may be aggravated by dairy.

(IBS), attention deficit disorder (ADD), attention deficit hyperactivity disorder (ADHD), and autism may be aggravated by dairy foods. Dairy reaction is not fully recognized by mainstream health professionals, although support and guidance are offered if individuals are obviously reacting to dairy.

In respect of ADD and ADHD in particular, there have been a number of case reports highlighting improvements in symptoms in a small number of children following a dairy-free diet. This of course does not apply to all children with ADD and ADHD, as scientists do not fully understand the link: further research is needed. It is therefore important to seek advice from a registered dietitian, and if possible a registered pediatric dietitian if you suspect that your child may be reacting to dairy foods.

Be totally reassured that you do not have to compromise at all on taste, variety, or pleasure in cooking and eating dairy-free. In fact, this should be seen as a new beginning—an opportunity to gain health benefits, and balance and optimize your diet as well as to introduce new ingredients and try a wide range of tasty recipes.

This book is for all people who are interested in dairy-free: for those following a strict dairy-free diet, a reduced dairy-free diet, or who are simply including more dairy-free options in their diet. It is designed to provide all the information, help, and advice you need, along with a rich variety of delicious dairy-free recipes for you, your family, and your friends to enjoy.

Reasons why people choose dairy-free

* Milk protein allergy
* Lactose intolerance
  * inherited
  * as a result of an intestinal infection and antibiotic use
  * as a result of intestinal surgery
  * as a result of a disease, such as celiac disease, affecting the lining of the intestines
  * as a result of malnutrition
* Religious reasons
* Moral reasons, such as veganism
* Dairy reaction—in some people symptoms associated with various conditions such as headaches, arthritis, IBS, eczema, autism, ADD and ADHD are aggravated by dairy
* Seeking a healthier lifestyle

what is lactose intolerance?

Lactose is a natural sugar found in human milk and the milk of other mammals, including goats and sheep. Lactose intolerance is not an allergic reaction. It occurs because the body lacks or produces an insufficient amount of an enzyme in our intestines called lactase.

Symptoms

During normal digestion, the lactase enzyme breaks down lactose into simpler sugars—glucose and galactose—so that the body can absorb it. If the body fails to produce enough lactase, the lactose passes through the intestines unprocessed into the lower intestines where the naturally present bacteria feed on it, giving off gas and causing pain, bloating, flatulence, and diarrhea.

Who is affected by lactose intolerance?

Lactose intolerance is estimated to affect around two thirds of the world's population. This condition is usually inherited and is more common among adolescents and adults, but in rare cases a child is born without the ability to make lactase. Some races, particularly those from Southeast Asia and the Middle East, parts of Africa, and India, are more susceptible to lactose intolerance because they do not normally drink milk after infancy, so the body stops producing the lactase enzyme. Some of these sufferers find they can tolerate a certain amount of milk and that if they persist

with drinking milk on a regular basis, the body begins to produce the enzyme again and their problems are overcome. In northern Europe, where dairy products are commonly eaten, people are less likely to have reduced levels of the lactase enzyme.

Lactose intolerance can also be brought on temporarily by malnutrition, a intestinal infection, intestinal surgery, or because a disease such as celiac disease has damaged the lining of the intestines.

How much milk causes symptoms?

The quantity of milk needed to cause symptoms varies widely. Some people with this intolerance can drink as much as a glass of milk a day without any problems and sometimes more. Others have to avoid it altogether. A doctor or registered dietitian or nutritionist will be able to advise you about your particular condition and it may be a case of trial and error to find out how much you can consume without reacting. Dairy products with a low lactose content, like hard cheese, butter, and yogurts with live cultures, can often be eaten by people who are lactose intolerant without any side effects. Some can tolerate an amount of goat's and sheep's milk, although these also contain lactose and can provoke a reaction. However, all the recipes in this book are completely dairy-free, so that they are suitable for every level of intolerance. If some dairy can be tolerated, the recipes can be adapted.

Diagnosis

Lactose intolerance may simply be diagnosed following detailed questioning by a doctor. It can also be diagnosed via a controlled food challenge (see page 14). Your doctor may be able to arrange for a lactose intolerance test or a "hydrogen breath test," which are other ways of detecting a lactose intolerance.

Foods containing lactose, including ingredients to watch for on food labels

* Cow's milk
* Goat's and sheep's milk
* Milk powder, milk solids
* Buttermilk
* Cheese, cheese powder, cheese flavoring
* Yogurt, yogurt with live cultures
* Butter and margarine (unless milk-free)
* Cream
* Ice cream
* Lactose (Milk sugar)
* Milk chocolate
* Hydrolyzed casein
* Whey, whey protein, whey syrup sweetener
* Certain low-calorie sweeteners
* Some brands of monosodium glutamate (MSG)

Other sources of lactose

* Medicines
* Dietary supplements, such as vitamin and mineral capsules
* Some toothpastes

about allergies

A food allergy is a more severe type of food intolerance, where the immune system reacts abnormally to a food or food substance. Normally our immune system acts as a defence mechanism, protecting the body from harmful substances such as viruses and bacteria, and thereby preventing ill health. In the allergic person there is a breakdown in the immune system, causing the body to react adversely to a normally harmless substance.

A traditional allergic response involves immune-system antibodies, known as IgE, and this happens very fast. In someone who has a dairy allergy, the body's antibodies are released in response to proteins in milk and almost immediately this triggers the release of histamine, producing an itchy inflammation. When someone's body produces high levels of IgE antibodies in response to an intake of common food proteins, such as those found in milk, this reaction is often an indication of later allergy to inhalants, such as dust and pollen.

Many different substances can cause an allergic reaction, which often makes it very difficult to pinpoint the offending substance. Certain foods, including milk and milk products, nuts, seeds, fish (especially shellfish), eggs, and wheat, are among the most common suspects in cases of food intolerance and allergy. Symptoms can be mild to severe, from discomfort to illness and, in the worst cases, death. An extreme reaction is referred to as an anaphylactic reaction. This is life-threatening and thankfully rare. If you or your child suffers from anaphylaxis, it is vital that you go to an allergy specialist clinic. It is also highly recommended that you get in touch with the The Food Allergy and Anaphylaxis Network for more detailed information (see page 140). It is important with all allergies to pinpoint which food or foods are causing the problem so that the correct action can be taken. Depending on the severity of the situation, this can mean eating less of the offending food or removing it from the diet altogether, temporarily or permanently.

What causes allergies?

The causes of allergies are not yet properly understood. A good deal of research is in progress investigating this complex and controversial subject. Allergies do appear to have a genetic link, so if there is a family history, children are more likely to suffer from an allergy, particularly if both parents have this disposition. In fact, the chances that a child will develop an allergy are two to five times greater if either or both parents have a history of allergies.

Are allergies on the increase?

The short answer to this question is yes, though allergies are also being reported and diagnosed more than in the past. Diagnosis is not straightforward, and cases may also go undetected and unrecorded, with sufferers simply accepting and living with the symptoms.

Increased press reports certainly seem to give the impression that food intolerance, and allergy in particular, is becoming more prevalent. This may be a consequence of 20th-century living: increased air pollution, more sterile environments, and more use of chemicals and pesticides. It has also been suggested that modern medicine has reduced our risk of infection so that our immune systems are not sufficiently challenged and, in genetically susceptible individuals, respond to ordinary harmless substances. However, we have little research to prove that this is the case.

A study recently published in the *Lancet* found that although 20 percent of adults thought they had some sort of food allergy, testing showed that only 3 percent actually did. The prevalence of proven IgE food allergy in young children is about 1–3 percent, and it is less in adults, at about 1 percent of the population. The proven prevalence of food intolerance in general is 5–8 percent in children and 1–2 percent in adults.

It may not be true that more of us have food intolerance, but rather that those that do are no longer suffering in silence. We may be more informed, better at recognizing symptoms, and more willing to actively seek help to discover what the problem is and how to alleviate it. Many of us are also much more aware of the effect that diet has on well-being.

Food allergy does not commonly develop for the first time in adults. An exception is a reaction to shellfish. This tends to develop in older people rather than children.

Can milk allergies be prevented?

A baby's digestive system is unable to cope with the composition of cow's milk, so it is recommended that regular cow's milk should not be introduced before a child is twelve months old. It is often when cow's milk is introduced, either as a modified formula milk or during weaning on to solid foods, that unpleasant symptoms arise. Some evidence suggests that exclusive breastfeeding for up to twelve months may offer some protection against cow's milk intolerance.

Cow's-milk protein-allergy

Milk allergy is an immune reaction to the protein (not the lactose) found in milk. Unlike lactose intolerance, it is uncommon. It is generally restricted to young children and nearly always develops following the introduction of formula milk into their diet. Symptoms include vomiting, diarrhea, and abdominal pain, as well as problems involving the skin, such as eczema, and breathing. In rare cases the reaction can be severe. It affects about 3–5 percent of children and usually clears up by the age of five years. Once cow's-milk protein-allergy has been diagnosed (see page 14), a complete dairy-free diet is recommended until such time that dairy may be reintroduced, as recommended by the doctor or registered dietitian. Sometimes children suffer from both milk allergy and lactose intolerance. This can occur particularly after a stomach upset.

diagnosis of dairy intolerances

If you suspect that you have a milk (or any other) intolerance, the first step is to visit your family doctor to ensure that your symptoms are not due to any other condition or illness. It really helps to take a food and symptom diary along with you (see right). A detailed examination of your general health, medical history, and food diary can lead to a diagnosis, but some tests may be required to confirm or investigate a possible diagnosis.

The medical profession varies in its attitude and approach to the treatment of allergies. You may be referred to a specialist unit or clinic for tests or referred to a registered specialist dietitian if dietary changes are considered.

A word on "dairy reaction"

Dairy reaction (see page 9) has a different effect on the body from that of lactose intolerance and cow's-milk protein-allergy. Instead of centering on IgE antibodies, it is identified by the presence of an antibody known as IgG which appears in days rather than minutes, and may well have the wide-ranging effects that sufferers claim. There is a variety of tests for this type of milk intolerance, the most common involving testing a pinprick of blood for IgG responses to a range of food proteins, including those found in milk. The tests are not as yet fully recognized by mainstream medicine, as the supporting scientific evidence is limited, but future research may highlight the benefits of IgG testing.

Recognized tests for allergies and intolerances

While the following tests are the most reliable ones currently available, most are not foolproof. It is often a combination of tests alongside the interpretation and advice of a skilled health professional that can lead to the best diagnosis.

The radio allergo sorbent test (RAST)
This test can be used for identifying acute allergies when there is an immediate reaction, by measuring IgE antibodies in the blood.

The skin-prick test
A few drops of a suspect allergen are put on the skin which is then pricked, so that the allergen seeps underneath. After a brief delay the doctor looks for signs of a reaction. This test is more successful for detecting environmental allergens, such as cat or dog hair which provoke an immediate reaction, and can be less useful for food allergies to which the reaction is often delayed.

Lactose tolerance test and hydrogen breath test
These can be used to confirm diagnosis of lactose intolerance. The lactose tolerance test measures the influence of lactose consumption on blood sugar levels, which can increase slightly if the lactose is not entirely digested. The hydrogen breath test measures the exhaled hydrogen after lactose consumption and is the more commonly used of the two methods. Raised hydrogen levels indicate the presence of undigested lactose because the intestinal bacteria ferment the undigested lactose and produce hydrogen, which is transported by the blood and released in the exhaled breath.

Exclusion and challenge diets
These are the most accurate and effective means of pinpointing a food intolerance. The process is straight-forward, although time-consuming. Suspect foods are excluded from the diet and then you wait to see if symptoms improve. The suspect foods are then gradually reintroduced to see if the symptoms return.

All exclusion diets should be carried out with the supervision of a registered dietitian or nutritionist to ensure a balanced intake, and advise on any necessary supplementation. Lifestyles vary and people have different dietary and medical requirements. A registered dietitian will be able to provide advice that is tailored to a particular situation and will be able to answer any specific questions. Exclusion diets should never be attempted with children or if there is any risk or history of anaphylaxis (see page 12), unless under strict supervision. Any exclusion diet must be followed for at least two weeks to see if there is a noticeable improvement. You need to stick to it faithfully and keep a food and symptom diary to record the results. It is best to choose a period when you have no social commitments and enough time to devote complete attention to what you are eating and drinking.

There are many ways of following an exclusion diet and the one you choose will depend on whether a single food is already suspected as the culprit or whether there is the potential of others.

It is important to fill the diary in throughout the day, as it is very hard to remember what was eaten after the event. Record absolutely everything eaten and drunk, including any medicines and supplements.

Simple exclusion diet
This type of diet involves excluding all sources of one type of food, such as milk and dairy products, for two to four weeks, and then assessing if there is any improvement.

Few foods/elimination diet
This type of diet is used when food intolerance is suspected but the culprits are unconfirmed and is generally appropriate when multiple food intolerance is suspected. It involves eating, for a recommended period of time, a very basic diet of only five to seven fresh foods, which are thought least likely to cause an allergic reaction. Other foods are then gradually reintroduced one by one so that the offending foods can be identified when symptoms occur. This diet can be very restrictive, sometimes boring, and time-consuming. However, it can be tremendously useful if multiple intolerances are suspected. The good news is that excluding just milk products need not be difficult, daunting, or tedious. The recipes in this book will give you lots of delicious options for enjoyable and nutritious menus.

Top tips when embarking on an elimination diet
Plan ahead and have the foods in the house that you need.
* Choose a time to start your diet that is easiest from a social point of view.
* Fill in your food and symptom diary as you go.
* Make an appointment to see your doctor and dietitian as soon as the diary is complete so that the experience is fresh in your mind.

If you are diagnosed with a cow's milk allergy, you will have to follow a completely dairy-free diet.

Non-medical-based allergy testing
Many places, including health food stores, offer a variety of so-called allergy testing methods. These include hair analysis, pulse tests, sweat tests, and kinesiology. However, they are unreliable and not recognized by the medical profession as having any scientific basis. They cost money and unfortunately result in many people unnecessarily following a complete dairy-free diet without expert guidance, often putting their nutrient intake and health at risk. Such a diet should be undertaken only on the advice of a qualified health professional.

Example of a food and symptom diary

Date	Time	Food and drink consumed	Symptoms	Time when symptoms experienced	Severity rating*
5 Jan.	7 a.m.	Oatmeal with milk Orange juice	Stomach cramps and diarrhea Feeling tired	9 a.m. All morning	3 4

* Rate your symptoms as follows: 1=mild, 2=moderate, 3=bad, 4=severe.

dairy-free and nutrition

What exactly are dairy foods?

Dairy foods include cow's milk and any food that is derived from it, such as cheese, cream, butter, and related items like buttermilk, yogurt, and ice cream. People following a dairy-free diet may or may not also have to avoid goat's and sheep's milk, depending on whether they are intolerant to these. Dairy is in many more foods than may at first be apparent—numerous processed foods contain milk and dairy products. Obvious examples include spreads and chocolate, but there are many more. A detailed list along with top tips and advice about what to look for on food labels is found on pages 22–23. The recipes in this book are all free from cow's, goat's, and sheep's milk and related products.

Is it healthy to avoid dairy?

Anyone wanting to start a strict dairy-free diet or even substantially reduce their dairy intake should first seek advice from a doctor or registered dietitian or nutritionist. Milk is one of the major foods in our diet, providing valuable amounts of protein, fat, and carbohydrate, as well as vitamins and minerals. It is a particularly good source of vitamins D, A, and B2, is rich in calcium, and a good source of phosphorus. For young children, milk is often a main provider of energy. If you give up dairy, it is therefore important to look at other ways of obtaining these nutrients, especially calcium.

There are alternative sources of all the nutrients that milk provides. Calcium is certainly one we should all focus on if removing significant amounts of dairy from the diet. Some of us may also need to think about alternative protein sources, but the other nutrients should not pose problems for most people, as long as they follow a varied diet. See page 28 for advice about a balanced intake. If you are unsure about certain nutrients, you should see a registered dietitian or nutritionist.

Why think about calcium?

Calcium is essential for healthy bones —it helps to give them their strength and density. Osteoporosis occurs when bones have lost so much of their mineral content that they become brittle and break easily. As dairy products are the main source of calcium in our diet, it is essential to replace this calcium if dairy is being significantly reduced or completely avoided.

Calcium is vital for young children and teenagers, but even after we stop growing at eighteen years, it remains very important in the diet. During pregnancy women should ensure that they are having enough calcium, and when breastfeeding they need extra.

Top tips for a good calcium intake and healthy bones
* Enjoy a balanced diet providing a wide range of nutrients.
* Get enough calcium: choose two or

Calcium content of various foods

7 fl.oz/(scant cup)/glass whole/lowfat/skim milk	237/248/249mg
7 fl.oz/(scant cup)/glass calcium-enriched soy milk	240–280mg
7 fl.oz/(scant cup)/glass calcium-fortified orange juice	245mg
1/2 cup cottage cheese	82mg
1oz (about 1/3 cup, shredded) hard cheese	216mg
2/3 cup lowfat yogurt	175mg
1/2 cup lowfat calcium-enriched soy yogurt	150mg
2 slices white/wholewheat bread	66/33mg
3 1/2 oz canned sardines with bones	460mg
1 orange	72mg
2/3 cup baked beans	80mg
12 almonds	62mg
2 tablespoons cooked spinach (about 3oz)	128mg

three servings of calcium-enriched dairy alternatives a day. Include other good sources such as greens, dairy-free bread, and canned fish with bones such as sardines. Some people need a supplement—but seek advice from a registered dietitian or nutritionist.

✱ Get enough vitamin D which helps with the absorption of calcium.

✱ Every day eat at least five portions of fruit and vegetables to supply you with potassium and other minerals which are also important for good bone health.

✱ When drinking alchohol, keep to sensible limits (see page 30).

✱ Stay active on a regular basis. Weight-bearing exercise (such as brisk walking, dancing, and aerobics) is particularly beneficial for optimum bone health.

Calcium requirements

Age	Calcium (mg/day)
Children	
0–12 months	525
1–3 years	350
4–6 years	450
7–10 years	550
Males	
11–18 years	1,000
19 years +	700
Females	
11–18 years	800
19 years +	700
Breastfeeding	Extra 550

Should I worry about protein?

The protein ordinarily obtained from milk and milk products such as cheese and yogurt can easily be obtained from other foods. Such foods include soy milk and soy products, poultry, fish, nuts, legumes (peas, beans, and lentils), and a combination of whole grains and vegetables. Only people who cannot take soy substitutes and have a low intake of animal foods might be at risk of insufficient protein in their diet. This can lead to poor growth development and repair of cells, and could happen when, for example, someone was using rice milk instead of cow's milk because they were allergic to soy and were also vegetarian. People in this situation should most certainly seek guidance from a registered dietitian and nutritionist who will be able to ensure a balanced intake and assess whether any supplementation may be necessary.

How much protein do we need per day?

The amount of protein needed in the daily diet varies according to age and sex. Generally adults require 45–53g (1½–2oz) per day. See the table on page 19 as a guide to the protein content of various foods, to give you an indication of how these protein needs can be met.

3½ oz skinless chicken breast, grilled = 32g

1 cup lowfat cow's milk = 8.2g

1 cup lowfat soy milk = 9.3g

Rice milk = 0.0g

1 medium slice wholewheat bread = 3.4g

1 medium slice white bread = 3g

12 almonds = 5.5g

1¾ cups white rice (cooked weight) = 4.7g

8oz macaroni (cooked weight) = 7g

2oz (average portion) boiled carrots = 0.4g

What about vitamin D?

The body makes its own vitamin D when exposed to sunlight. This exposure is our main source of vitamin D. In northern countries it is recommended that you expose your skin to the daylight for 10–20 minutes every day between early spring and mid-autumn, but avoid sun exposure between the hours of 12 p.m. and 3 p.m. in the summer months. In addition, egg yolk and fish, particularly fish liver oils, are good sources of vitamin D. There are small quantities in carrots, pumpkins, sweet potatoes, apricots, squash, broccoli, spinach, and other dark leafy greens.

Milk substitutes

Calcium-enriched soy milk and yogurt should ideally be the main substitutes for dairy milk and yogurt as they have the best nutrient profile. Soy's protein quality is equivalent to that of meat, milk, and eggs, which are the main protein sources in our diet. Rice milk is normally advised for those who cannot take soy.

Generally speaking, as long as people choose calcium-enriched soy milks and yogurts for dairy products, they should not suffer from a nutritional point of view. If using rice milk, a calcium-enriched variety should be chosen and it is also important to ensure that there is enough protein in the diet. Rice milk provides little more than water and added calcium, so when using rice milk in a recipe, always include a good protein source such as meat or legumes.

Other cow's milk substitutes include nut milks, goat's and sheep's milk, and lactose-reduced milks. However, their nutrient level may be much less than that of dairy or soy milks or they may contain a certain amount of lactose.

Adding soy to your shopping cart can benefit your health

＊ It has recently been recognized that eating soy foods on a regular basis helps to lower blood cholesterol. This is good news when we consider that more than 34 million American adults have raised cholesterol levels that could increase their risk of coronary heart disease.

＊ Soy protein is the active cholesterol-lowering ingredient in the soy bean. It has been proved that consuming 25g (about 1oz) of soy protein a day as part of a low-saturated-fat diet will help to lower blood cholesterol.

＊ Achieving your 25g daily intake of soy protein is easy. Simply include two 8 fl.oz glasses of soy milk and 1 cup of soy yogurt as part of your daily low-saturated-fat diet, or alternatively, use tofu in a stir-fry and include 1 cup of soy milk in a fruit smoothie or on your cereal, and in tea throughout the day. Do note however that the amount of soy protein in soy cream is negligible.

＊ The recipes in this book which include soy have been labeled according to how much soy protein they contain, which can help you assess if you are having 25g per day.

＊ Some women find that soy can help reduce unpleasant symptoms of the menopause. Those who suffer from severe hot flashes benefit the most.

＊ Soy is very nutritious and is one of the few sources of high-quality complete protein equivalent to that found in meat, dairy produce, and eggs, making it a useful food for all the family.

＊ Soy products have significantly changed over the years. As a food choice these days they are not only healthy but a tasty food, too—far removed from some of the strange options that were available in the past.

If you've never tried soy products before or haven't tasted them for a long time, then prepare to be pleasantly surprised! ✦ Including more soy in your diet follows Eastern ways of eating, in which dairy foods hardly feature. Indeed, around half of the recipes in this book have a Thai influence, but we have also included more traditional Western-type dishes with soy milk substitutes for the usual dairy products.

Taste and availability of dairy-free

The greatly improved taste and increased availability of dairy alternatives have certainly made it easy and more enjoyable to include them in our daily diet. Several years ago these foods were mostly confined to health food stores, with limited supplies found somewhere in the back of only a few supermarkets. Today they are available in all supermarkets and are highly visible alongside the dairy equivalents.

The increased popularity of dairy alternatives is reflected not only on the supermarket shelves but in restaurants and cafes, too. When we ask for a cappuccino, we are now commonly given the choice of a soy or other dairy-free version—something quite unheard of a couple of years ago.

Whatever the reason for omitting dairy from your meal or diet, one thing is for sure: you can still enjoy a wide range of varied and delicious meals.

Nutrient comparison of calcium-enriched soy milk and lowfat cow's milk

Nutrition per 100ml (3½ fl.oz)	Calcium-enriched soy milk	Lowfat cow's milk
Calories	47	47
Protein	3.8g	3.4g
Fat	2.2g	1.7g
Saturated	0.4g	1.1g
Polyunsaturated	1.4g	0g
Monounsaturated	0.5g	0.4g
Essential fatty acids		
Linoleic acid	58%	0%
Alpha linolenic acid	8%	0%
Carbohydrates	2.8g	5.2g
Lactose	0g	5.2g
Cholesterol	0g	7mg
Calcium	120–140mg	124mg

dairy foods to avoid

Depending on how strict your dairy-free diet needs to be, it may be necessary to avoid all of the following foods and ingredients or just some of them. Always check the labels carefully as products vary from brand to brand.

Dairy foods

* Fresh cow's milk—skim, lowfat and whole
* Canned condensed, evaporated, and dry/powdered cow's milk
* Buttermilk
* Cream
* Crème fraîche
* Quark
* Butter
* Cheese
* Yogurt
* Ice cream

Processed foods that may contain dairy

Many people do not realize how many foods actually contain quantities of dairy—chocolate is one and it is easy to underestimate how much dairy you are really eating.

Vegetables
* Vegetables canned in sauce containing milk or milk products: for example, creamed corn
* Instant mashed potato

Bread and baked goods
* Most bread
* Most cookies
* Some crackers
* Doughnuts
* Scones and oven biscuits
* Many cakes
* Many baking mixes

Cereals and grains
* Most types of muesli and many breakfast cereals now contain some dairy ingredients, particularly skim milk powder

Confectionery and snack foods
* Milk chocolate and some dark chocolate
* Fudge
* Toffee
* Butterscotch
* Many other candies
* Roasted nuts with a lactose-containing flavoring or milk-chocolate covering
* A number of potato chip brands, especially flavored varieties

Desserts
* Most instant desserts
* Most traditional pudding types
* Canned rice pudding
* Batter mixes and pancakes
* Cheesecakes
* Mousses
* Custards

Savory foods
* Many soups
* Creamy sauces
* Dips based on yogurt or cheese
* Salad dressings made with milk or milk products
* Certain store-bought gravies

* Quiches and flans
* Many pre-prepared supermarket meals
* Crumbed and battered foods
* Some sausages and other processed meats: for example, some hams
* Some pies, sausage rolls, and pastries
* Pizzas
* Lasagnas
* Many pasta dishes
* Some waffles

Beverages
* Coffee whitener
* Milkshakes
* Many fruit smoothie drinks
* Malted milk drinks, such as Horlicks, Ovaltine, and Bournvita
* Vending-machine tea
* Instant hot chocolate drinks (cocoa is usually dairy-free)
* Cream-based liqueurs and cocktails

Spreads, fats, and oils
* Dairy spreads
* Most brands of margarine contain some buttermilk, skim milk, or whey powder
* Low- or reduced-fat spreads can contain buttermilk
* Most lemon curd
* Chocolate spread

Miscellaneous
* Monosodium glutamate (the flavor enhancer) containing lactose
* Some bouillon cubes
* Tablets containing a lactose filler
* Toothpaste containing a lactose filler
* Low-calorie sweeteners containing lactose

Hidden dairy ingredients

Apart from the obvious dairy ingredients listed above, milk products appear in numerous guises in many processed foods, from batters to biscuits and margarines to medicines. For instance, cow's-milk protein may be included in foods in the form of casein or whey, and many people do not realize that these are derived from cow's milk. Watch out for the following terms in the lists of ingredients on food packaging.

Terms used by manufacturers that indicate the presence of cow's milk

* Butter listed as fat, flavoring, oil, or solids
* Casein, hydrolyzed casein, rennet casein
* Caseinates (ammonium, calcium, magnesium, potassium, sodium)
* Curds
* Dried milk (nonfat milk powder)
* Dry milk solids
* Hydrolyzed milk protein
* Lactalbumin, lactalbumin phosphate
* Lactate

* Lactoferrin
* Lactoglobulin
* Lactose
* Milk derivative fat/solids
* Opta (fat replacer)
* Simplesse (fat replacer)
* Sour cream solids/milk solids
* Whey, delactosed whey, demineralized whey, sweet whey powder, whey powder, whey protein concentrate, whey solids

Food preparation and contamination

Depending on how strict your diet has to be, you may need to think about possible sources of contamination: for instance, having french fries from a restaurant fried in oil which may have previously been used to fry a battered food; or eating non-dairy cheese from a cheeseboard shared with dairy cheese and cut with the same knife.

If you suffer from a severe food allergy it is important to gain advice from a specialist on food preparation and contamination from food allergy clinics, as well as specialist organizations such as The Food Allergy and Anaphylaxis Network (see page 140 for details).

Traps for the unwary: foods in which it is not obvious that cow's milk may be present

Soy cheese
Goat cheese
Vegetarian cheese
Margarine and lowfat spreads
Bread
Cookies and cakes
Sausages
Rusks (Zwieback)
Non-milk-fat ice cream
Instant mashed potato
Muesli and many breakfast cereals
Dried and canned soups
Fish coated in batter

dairy alternatives

A totally dairy-free diet involves the complete avoidance of cow's, goat's, and sheep's milk; milk products such as butter, cheese, cream, and yogurt; milk derivatives such as casein, whey, hydrolyzed whey, and non-fat milk solids; and lactose (milk sugar). Lactose is found in many foods as well as being used by the pharmaceutical industry as a filler in some tablets. All dairy alternatives listed below are suitable for those with cow's-milk protein-allergy as well as lactose intolerance. Goat's and sheep's milk may be tolerated in the diet of some cases of cow's-milk protein-allergy, but because they also contain some lactose, they are generally unsuitable for people with lactose intolerance.

Many supermarkets now regularly produce a list of milk-free manufactured foods. All supermarkets offer a customer service telephone number which you can call for this kind of information but it must be remembered that this rapidly becomes out of date owing to changes in the formulation of foods and the introduction of new products.

Dairy-free foods

It is impossible to give a "safe" list, so it is crucial always to check the ingredients on the packaging of manufactured brands of food for the presence of milk or milk derivatives. Below is a list of items that can generally be eaten safely (but still always read the label!) and it can be used as a general shopping list.

Fruit and vegetables
* Fruit (fresh, canned, and frozen)
* Fruit juices (fresh, frozen, canned, bottled, and UHT)
* Vegetables (fresh, frozen, dried)
* Certain brands of canned baked beans
* Certain brands of instant mashed potatoes

Meat and meat alternatives
* Fresh meat, poultry, game, bacon, and variety meats—not processed
* Most burgers and sausages—but check the label

Fish and fish products
* Fresh or frozen fish without batter or crumb coating
* Canned fish in brine, oil, or water
* Smoked plain fish
* Certain brands of fish sticks

Bread and baked goods
* Certain pita breads, muffins, and bagels—check the ingredients
* Some pastries and fruit pies—check the ingredients
* Meringues
* Homemade cakes and cookies made with milk-free ingredients, and certain store-bought brands—check the ingredients

Baking ingredients
* Baking powder
* Fresh and dried yeast
* Most flours
* Certain brands of custard powder

* Most plain dark chocolate
* Dried coconut
* Dried fruit
* Pastry—if made with pure vegetable fat
* Marzipan

Cereals and grains
* Rolled oats
* Certain brands of breakfast cereal such as Rice Krispies, some cornflakes (plain), Shredded Wheat (plain)
* Pasta, macaroni, couscous, rice, and other grains such as bulghur, quinoa

Confectionery, preserves, and snack foods
* Some dark chocolates, jelly candies, and hard candies
* Carob
* Sugar, glucose, jam, honey, molasses, marmalade, and certain brands of lemon curd
* Plain popsicles, most sorbets and most jellos
* Nuts
* Pretzels
* Some potato chips
* Most cream crackers and water biscuits
* Some oatcakes, rice cakes, and crispbreads

Soups
* Minestrone, lentil, oxtail, vegetable, and French onion—but check the ingredients

Sauces

* Mustard
* Some soy sauces
* Most tomato ketchups and pastes
* Most relishes and chutneys
* Certain brands of gravy granules

Dips

* Hummus
* Fresh tomato salsa

Beverages

* Fresh fruit juices
* The majority of soft drinks—but check the ingredients
* Tea (black)
* Coffee (black)
* Cocoa (without milk)
* Certain brands of drinking chocolate
* Most sodas

Spreads, fats, and oils

* Vegan margarine, pure soy spread, kosher margarine, beef and vegetable lard
* All pure vegetable and nut oils
* Vinaigrette dressing, mayonnaise, and salad dressing
* Most brands of peanut butter

Miscellaneous

* Salt
* Pepper
* Herbs and spices
* Vinegar
* Wines, liquors, and beers (caution should be taken with some liqueurs and cocktails)

Milk and dairy substitutes

A wide range of milk substitutes is now available in all supermarkets as well as health food stores and many local convenience stores. These can be used to replace regular cow's milk in drinks, on cereal, and in all recipes.

A form of cow's milk that may be tolerated

Lactose-reduced milk is made from cow's milk, but has a reduced lactose content through the addition of a natural lactase enzyme, similar to that found in our digestive system. This milk is available in long-life form and is generally a whole-milk product. It can be used by people with lactose intolerance who can tolerate some dairy.

Soy milks and soy drinks

Soy milk is the obvious choice for most people as a substitute for cow's milk—unless they are also allergic to soy protein. Made from soy beans, soy milk is widely available freshly chilled or in long-life form, sweetened or unsweetened, and in various flavors. It is more often than not fortified with calcium. It may also have some added vitamins. Soy drinks are lactose-free, cow's-milk protein-free, and generally low in fat with an equivalent fat content to that of lowfat cow's milk, although more rarely some nonfat and whole-milk versions are available. The plain sweetened options are sweetened to the level of cow's milk, and are therefore easily accepted by the palate when you are first making the switch. However, in the long run, it is worth considering the unsweetened options, as they will be kinder to your dental health.

Plain soy milk can be used as a complete milk replacement on cereals as well as in hot drinks such as tea and cappuccino, and in all kinds of recipes. Surprisingly, it has a more creamy flavor than lowfat cow's milk, even though it is low in fat. No soy milk to date can be used with regular coffee as it tends to curdle.

Approximately 80 percent of people allergic to cow's milk can tolerate soy, but some allergic individuals may react to soy protein as well as to goat's and sheep's milk protein.

Regular soy milks should not be introduced as a main milk source for children under two years of age. Calcium-enriched varieties can be used from six months in cooking but not as a main milk source.

Coconut milk and cream

Coconut milk makes a tasty substitute for dairy in many recipes and goes particularly well in Thai dishes including the ones in this book. However, it is one of the few vegetable foods that is high in saturated fat—the type of fat more commonly found to be high in animal foods such as whole-milk and cheese—and we should all be having less of it. Try not to use coconut milk too often, and dilute with water or use the reduced-fat version if you want to lower the fat content but keep the taste.

Goat's and sheep's milk

Both goat's and sheep's milk contain lactose and so are unsuitable for anyone with more than a mild intolerance to lactose. These types of milk can also provoke a reaction in allergic individuals. Their protein content is similar to that of cow's milk, though not identical. Goat's milk is deficient in folic acid, so if it is chosen regularly, the user should ensure a good intake of folic acid from other sources including green leafy vegetables and whole grain foods.

Goat's and sheep's milk are both as versatile as cow's milk. Goat's milk has a much stronger taste than cow's milk and sheep's milk has a higher fat content, which makes it taste creamier and richer. It is also sweeter than cow's milk.

These milks are not recommended for children under 2 years as a main milk source.

Rice milk

Rice milk is generally made from filtered water, rice syrup, vegetable oil, and various flavorings. Some types now have added calcium as it otherwise contains no calcium. It is lactose-free, low in fat, and contains a negligible or very small amount of protein.

Oat drink

Usually made from whole oats, vegetable oil, and filtered water, oat drink is lactose-free, low in fat, and contains a negligible or very small amount of protein.

Yogurts, desserts and ice cream

Regular cow's milk yogurt is a fermented milk food which may contain bacteria with enzymes that can digest the lactose in milk to produce lactic acid. It is therefore lower in lactose than milk and may be tolerated by people with mild lactose intolerance.

If goat's or sheep's milk can be tolerated by those with mild lactose intolerance, yogurts made from these milks are an option. They can now be found in some of the larger supermarkets and health food stores.

For people requiring a completely dairy-free alternative, there is a wide range of tasty soy yogurts, desserts, and ice cream available.

Creams

Soy cream is widely obtainable in the UK as a long-life alternative to light dairy cream, but as of this writing, it is not available in the US.

Goat's cream is available from larger supermarkets and health food stores. It has a sweet taste and can be used as a pouring cream or whipped cream in recipes.

Cheeses

Hard cheeses like cheddar and Parmesan are relatively low in lactose, enabling small amounts to be tolerated by those with a mild lactose intolerance. There is a relatively widely available selection of good-tasting goat cheeses and sheep's milk cheeses which can also be used easily in cooking. However, some brands can include cow's milk, so it is important to read the label. Alternatively there is a number of cheeses made from soy, mostly available from health food stores. These are the only soy foods which, to date, do not tend to taste as good as their dairy counterparts—they are often rather mild and rubbery. They also tend not to melt in the same way as dairy cheese.

Fats and spreads

Vegetable margarines and spreads often contain some whey or buttermilk which is added for flavor but makes them unsuitable for a dairy-free diet. It is important to choose from the dairy-free soy, kosher, or vegan spreads, or to use pure vegetable fats and oils. All can be used for spreading and in cooking.

Tofu

Tofu is a high-protein lowfat food made from soy beans. A fermented soy bean curd, it comes in a block which can have a firm or soft (silken) texture and is available plain, marinated, or smoked. Tofu is a good source of calcium and protein and is extremely versatile: it can be used in a wide variety of dishes, both sweet and savory. Silken tofu is creamy and good for dips, sauces, and toppings. Firm tofu can be marinated and used instead of cheese or meat.

choosing a balanced diet

Enjoying a balanced diet is important for everyone, which of course includes those following a dairy-free diet. Healthy food not only tastes good but it affects our mood and behavior too, making us all feel better and more alert, as well as boosting our energy levels. Eating healthily helps us all to get the most from life. Furthermore, eating well reduces our risk of many health problems, including heart disease, diabetes, and cancer.

A balanced diet should include a wide variety of foods from all five food groups every day. These are listed opposite in the table. Please note that this is a general guide and is not meant for children under five years of age, who have different dietary needs.

Fluid intake

Many of us do not think about our fluid consumption—it often takes second place to food. However, it is equally important. Around two thirds of the human body is made up of fluid. This is constantly lost or used up daily as we breathe, sweat, and go to the toilet. If we have an insufficient fluid intake, we cannot concentrate 100 percent and will not be as alert as we could be. We will also be increasing our chances of ill health as we will not be sufficiently clearing all the toxins from our body. Most people need at least 2 quarts of fluid a day—about 8 glasses—but more is required in hot weather and when exercising. A good way of telling if you

Choosing healthy food from the five main groups

Food group	Main nutrients provided	What to choose?	How much?
Potatoes, rice, bread, cereals, pasta, and other grains	Carbohydrate, fiber, B vitamins, potassium, some protein, some iron, some calcium, vitamin E, phytochemicals (natural plant elements)	Rice, potatoes, pasta, noodles, dairy-free crackers/bread, dairy-free breakfast cereals	5–14 portions daily 1 portion is: 3 tablespoons breakfast cereal 1 slice bread/fruit bread/ mini pita 1/2 breadroll/bun 1/2 scone/small pancake/waffle 2 egg-sized potatoes 3 tablespoons boiled pasta 2 heaped tablespoons boiled rice
Fruit and vegetables	Vitamin C, folic acid, potassium, fiber, beta carotene, some calcium, some iron, magnesium, some carbohydrate	All types—fresh, frozen, canned, dried; fresh juices	5 or more daily 1 portion is: 1 piece of regular fresh fruit, e.g. 1 orange, 1 banana 2 small fruit, e.g. 2 kiwis, 2 plums 2 tablespoons stewed or canned fruit 1 small glass (7fl.oz) fruit juice 1 tablespoon dried fruit
Dairy alternatives	Calcium, protein, vitamins A, D, B2, and B12, zinc, phosphorus (phytochemicals in plant-based options)	Lower-fat versions: lowfat calcium-enriched soy milks and yogurts	2–3 portions daily 1 portion is: 7fl.oz calcium-enriched dairy alternative 1/2 cup calcium-enriched yogurt alternative 1oz dairy-free soy cheese
Meat, fish, and alternatives	Protein, iron, zinc, magnesium, potassium (phytochemicals in peas, beans, lentils, and tofu options), essential fats from fatty fish options	Lean meats, poultry, fish, eggs, beans, peas, lentils, nuts, meat substitutes	2–4 portions daily 1 portion is: 2–2 1/2 oz beef, pork, ham, lamb, liver, kidney, chicken, fish 2 eggs 1/3 cup cooked beans (such as kidney or aduki) 1/4 cup cooked lentils 2 tablespoons nuts
Foods rich in fat and/or sugar	Fat, including some essential fats, sugar, vitamins, minerals	Vegetable oils such as olive, canola, soy and their spreads, lowfat dairy-free dressings	Eat in small amounts. Keep sugary foods and beverages to mealtimes to help reduce risk of tooth decay.

are drinking enough is to check the color of your urine. It should be a light straw color. If it is brown and smelly, you need to drink more.

Alcohol

Too much alcohol can damage the heart muscle, increase blood pressure, and also lead to weight gain. However, a sensible amount of alcohol on a regular basis can be good for our health. In the US, the current daily recommended intake is no more than 3 "units" for women and 4 "units" for men. A unit is equivalent to:

✱ 10fl.oz beer, stout (such as Guiness), cider
✱ 1 small (1/2 cup) glass of wine
✱ 1 shot (2 tbsp.) of liquor
✱ 2fl.oz (1/4 cup) glass of sherry or port
Avoid milky liqueurs and cocktails.

Salt

A certain amount of salt each day is essential, but it is important to watch our intake. Most of us eat far too much salt just because we've gotten used to eating far too much salt. As in the case of sugar, if we reduce our salt intake gradually, our tastebuds will adapt. Salt intake should not exceed 6g per day, equivalent to 1 1/2 level teaspoons fine salt or 2 1/4 teaspoons coarse salt. When cooking and at the table, try to limit the amount of salt you add, or skip it altogether. You will be surprised at how well your palate adjusts and how soon you won't like salty foods. When shopping and cooking, check food labels; if salt is listed as sodium, convert to grams of salt by multiplying the sodium value by 0.002.5.

And don't forget to keep moving…

With our sedentary lifestyles, most of us do not exercise nearly enough. This not only increases our chances of ill health but also affects our mood. It is amazing how a small amount of regular activity can change your outlook on life. It is currently recommended that every day we all do at least thirty minutes, and up to one hour, of activity or the equivalent of taking 10,000 steps! The key to regular exercise is to build up the habit.

Finally… get label happy!

Whatever type of diet you may be following (and if you are not following one but want to eat healthily), you need to watch your consumption of fat, sugar, and salt. It is often confusing trying to determine which foods are low in fat, sugar, and salt and also high in fiber. However, the simple guidelines below can make this assessment much easier. When reading food labels, check the amounts of fat, sodium, fiber, and sugar listed per serving, and compare with the recommended daily intake guide, below.

How many calories a day do I need?

The table below is a rough guide to the recommended daily amounts of calories and nutrients for an average man and woman. Use this information to help you make sense of food labels. For example, if a frozen meal contains 50g of fat, you know that it has over half the recommended amount of fat for the day.

Reading the ingredients label

If following a completely dairy-free diet, it is vital that you read the ingredients labels of all processed and convenience foods before purchasing them. By law,

In one serving, how much is a lot?	
A lot	**A little**
10g sugar	2g sugar
20g fat	3g fat
5g saturated fat	1g saturated fat
3g fiber	0.5g fiber
500mg sodium	100mg sodium
(or 1.25g salt)	(or 0.25g salt)

Recommended daily calorie and nutrient intake		
	Men	**Women**
Energy (calories)	2,500	2,000
Total Fat	80g	65g
Sat Fat	25g	20g
Cholesterol	300mg	300mg
Sodium	2,400mg	2,400mg
Total carbohydrate	375g	300g
Fiber	20g	16g

Nutrition Facts

Serving Size	8 Cookies (30g)
Servings Per Container	About 11

Amount per serving

Calories 140	Calories from Fat 50

	% Daily Value *
Total Fat 6g	9%
Saturated Fat 2g	10%
Trans Fat 0g	
Cholesterol 0mg	
Sodium 120mg	5%
Total Carbohydrate 21g	7%
Dietary Fiber less than 1g	1%
Sugars 9g	
Protein 1g	

Vitamin A 0%	Vitamin C 0%
Calcium 0%	Iron 0%

* Percent Daily Values are based on a 2,000 calorie diet. Your daily values may be higher or lower depending on your calorie needs:

Calories	2,000	2,500
Total Fat	65g	80g
Sat Fat	20g	25g
Cholesterol	300mg	300mg
Sodium	2,400mg	2,400mg
Total Carbohydrate	300g	375g
Dietary Fiber	25g	30g

CONTAINS: WHEAT, MILK AND SOY INGREDIENTS

INGREDIENTS: ENRICHED FLOUR (WHEAT FLOUR, NIACIN, REDUCED IRON, THIAMIN MONONITRATE [VITAMIN B₁], RIBOFLAVIN [VITAMIN B₂], FOLIC ACID), SUGAR, VEGETABLE OIL (SOYBEAN, PALM AND PALM KERNEL OIL WITH TBHQ FOR FRESHNESS), CONTAINS TWO PERCENT OR LESS OF SALT, HIGH FRUCTOSE CORN SYRUP, NATURAL AND ARTIFICIAL FLAVOR, LEAVENING (BAKING SODA, MONOCALCIUM PHOSPHATE), BUTTER (CREAM, SALT), SOY LECITHIN.

food labels must list all the ingredients in order of weight and lists can be quite lengthy. It may seem time-consuming examining labels, but it becomes easier when you are only checking for any changes in the ingredients of foods you are already familiar with.

What if there is no label?

There is no legal requirement for loose unpackaged foods to have a list of ingredients. If you need to know more about such food products as bread fresh from the bakery, ask the shop assistant who should have access to a product information guide.

Product changes

Manufacturers change their ingredients from time to time to improve a recipe or because they have changed their supplier, so it's best not to assume that a product is safe to eat simply because you have bought it before—be sure to always check the label.

dairy-free shopping and cooking

Preparing for your first dairy-free shopping trip may seem daunting at first. However, with the wide variety of foods now available in supermarkets and the ever-increasing choice of dairy-free products, you will be surprised at how quickly you will adjust both to shopping and preparing your food.

To begin with, use the list of dairy-free foods on page 25 as the basis for a good shopping list. Most major supermarkets produce a list of their dairy-free branded foods which will also help with shopping and getting used to the foods you can safely enjoy. A number of supermarkets also have their own "free from" range of foods where dairy-free foods may now all be found in one section. Many supermarkets have their own customer careline which you can phone for detailed information about products. Look out also for the manufacturer's careline number on the label of branded foods.

Changing your diet provides you with a great opportunity to focus on what you are eating, to go back to basics and follow a really healthy eating regime. Stock up on a wide variety of foods from all the major food groups as highlighted on page 29. Stock your fridge and freezer with fish, chicken, eggs, lean meat, fruit, fresh and frozen vegetables, and dairy-free alternatives to milk, yogurt, cheese, and so on. It is important to have a plentiful supply of dairy-free beverages that you enjoy, from water to tea, fruit juices, and dairy-alternative milks (the calcium-enriched varieties). It might also be a good time, depending on how much you have cooked in the past, to think about healthy cooking equipment.

Healthy cooking equipment
* Nonstick pans
* Wok
* Steamer
* Pressure cooker
* Food processor
* Vegetable scrubber and peeler
* Juicer

Stocking your cupboard
Use the following list to help you fill your cupboard with healthy dairy-free ingredients:
* Dairy-free breakfast cereals such as rolled oats and shredded wheat
* Fresh calcium-enriched soy milk and cream, soy cheese and yogurts
* Fresh vegetables, e.g. sweet potatoes, peppers, broccoli, tomatoes, onions, eggplants, chilies, pumpkin, snow peas, carrots, scallions, frozen peas
* Fresh fruit, e.g. pears, apples, bananas, lemons, limes, lychees, mangoes
* Herbs, e.g. cilantro, mint, parsley
* Pasta, rice, and noodles, e.g. fettuccine, macaroni, rice noodles, basmati rice, risotto rice
* Popcorn, plain nuts and seeds, e.g. roasted peanuts, pine nuts, slivered almonds, walnuts, sesame seeds
* Wholewheat flour, all-purpose white flour, rice flour
* Buckwheat, couscous, cornmeal
* Dried fruit: apricots, prunes, raisins, and golden raisins
* Canned or dried beans, peas, and lentils
* Canned fruit in natural juice
* Canned tomatoes, corn, bamboo shoots
* Canned salmon, mackerel, tuna, and sardines in brine
* Tofu
* Garlic, ginger, chilies, lemongrass, olives, vinegars, Thai fish sauce, dairy-free soy sauces—light and dark, dairy-free bottled ketchup and mustards, honey
* Spices, e.g. chili powder, curry paste, turmeric powder, cumin seeds, ground cinnamon
* Olive, peanut, canola, sesame, and chili oils
* Chicken, beef, and vegetable bouillon cubes
* Ready-made long-life low-fat soy custard

Dairy-free cooking

Dairy substitutes such as soy milk can be used as a straight swap for cow's milk on cereals, in tea, and in numerous recipes from sauces, soups, and other savory dishes, to puddings and cakes. (See page 26 for more information). All the inspiration you need for healthy, dairy-free cooking is provided by the recipes later on in this book. They offer plenty of delicious options for the whole family and for every occasion.

Suggested menu plans for healthy dairy-free eating

	Menu 1	Menu 2	Menu 3	Menu 4	Menu 5
Breakfast	Mango Smoothie (see page 138) Oatmeal with Honey (see page 47)	Fresh orange juice Luxury Breakfast Muesli (see page 44)	Warm Prunes with Coconut and Orange Zest (see page 48) Slice of wholewheat toast with yeast spread Lemongrass Hot Drink (page 138)	Apple juice Coconut Crêpes with Banana and Maple Syrup (see page 44)	Fresh orange juice Fried Rice with Ham and Peas topped with Poached Egg (see page 49)
Lunch	Carrot and Sweet Potato soup (see page 72) Chunky soda bread	Grilled Salmon Steaks with Creamy Lemon Sauce (see page 85) Green salad	Stuffed Peppers with Aromatic Rice (see page 96)	Shredded Omelet in Mild Broth (see page 75) Chunky wholewheat roll	Spicy Triple-flavor Noodle Soup with Broccoli and Bean sprouts (see page 74)
Evening meal	Baked Marinated Sea Bass with Mashed Sweet Potatoes (see page 85) Pear Crumble (see page 129)	Carrot and Pumpkin Risotto (see page 98) Spicy Chilled Cucumber and Ham Salad (see page 67)	Grilled Lamb Chops with Fresh Peppercorns, Cilantro Roots, and Shallots (see page 120) Grated carrot Green salad Watermelon Ice (see page 137)	Vegetable Lasagna (see page 106) Baked Apples with Walnuts and Custard (see page 129)	Chicken and Vegetables with Cashews and Roasted Dried Chilies (see page 116) Asian Fruit Salad (see page 126)

It is best not to have a dessert every day, though this is dependent on your weight and calorie requirements. One or two desserts per week is generally fine if you are looking to maintain your weight. On other days, choose a favorite fruit instead.

feeding children

Babies

If there is a history of severe food allergy in the family, it is best for the mother to avoid that food when breastfeeding: in this case, specialist advice should be sought. If children are going to develop a milk allergy, it usually happens in the first year of life and when cow's milk formula is introduced; they should grow out of it by three to five years of age. Lactose intolerance more often occurs later, in adult life. All mothers are encouraged to breastfeed exclusively for up to twelve months, if possible, and to start weaning from this time. Among other benefits, this is thought to help prevent allergy, and can be particularly beneficial where there is a family history of allergies. It is a relatively new recommendation: the advice formerly given was to breastfeed exclusively until six months and start weaning then. In practice, some babies appear to need weaning after six months. This is certainly something that should be discussed with your health visitor, registered dietitian, or doctor, who can take your baby's individual health and medical details into account.

If your baby is diagnosed with cow's-milk protein-allergy, expert advice from a registered dietitian will be essential. Once the dairy-free diet commences, your child will return to being a happy healthy youngster. If you are not breastfeeding, you may be advised to feed your baby a hydrolyzed milk formula (in which the cow's milk protein is broken down to its most basic form). In some cases, a

soy infant formula may also be recommended. Individual and specific advice will then be provided by your dietitian for following a dairy-free weaning process.

Young children

A healthy diet is essential for normal growth as well as physical and mental development. If healthy eating habits are formed young enough, these will be carried through to adult life. Taking a child off an important food group like dairy foods is safe as long as they are replaced with healthy alternatives like calcium-enriched soy drinks, yogurts, and so on.

Once children get close to school age, they will notice if they have to do something different from their friends. Children do not like to be different from their peers, so it is important not to make an issue about any special dietary needs. Unfortunately, many of the dairy foods that need to be avoided—such as puddings, ice cream, chocolate, and custard—are favorites among children. This is why it is so important to provide enjoyable alternatives.

Breakfast
It sounds like a cliché but this is the most important meal of the day. Consistently going without breakfast places a child at significant risk of poor nutrition as their growing body will potentially be missing out on a third of its needs. A child who is poorly nourished will also be less alert, and

less able to concentrate at school, and more tired overall. Invest in providing enough time to eat in the morning and to help encourage lifetime habits—try to make it fun. Breakfast can easily be boring if it is always the same. Buy or prepare a variety of healthy cereals and baked foods like muffins and bagels, and stock up on a range of fresh calcium-enriched yogurt alternatives, drinks, and favorite canned fruit in natural juice. Pureed apple is a hit with young children; it can be made the night before, or a larger quantity can be prepared in advance and frozen in small amounts which can then be thawed as needed in the fridge overnight.

Breakfast suggestions
* Oatmeal with Honey (see page 47) and Mango Smoothie (see page 138)
* Warm Prunes with Coconut and Orange Zest (see page 48) with dairy-free muesli
* Fried Rice with Ham and Peas topped with Poached Egg (page 49)

School dinners
Always make sure the school knows about any special dietary needs. If necessary, arrange a meeting with the caterer who will be able to advise on specific recipe ingredients and alternative options. Here are some suggestions for dairy-free school dinners:
* Baked potato without butter, topped with tuna or baked beans
* Sweet-and-sour chicken with rice
* Roast chicken, potatoes, and vegetables

* Spaghetti with meatballs
* Lamb stew and potatoes
* Shepherd's pie—chopped leftover lamb and gravy baked with a mashed potato topping (the mashed potato made with soy milk and vegan spread)

Dessert could be one of the following:
* Fruit
* Fruit jello
* Fruit crumble
* Lemon meringue pie
* Oat bar
* Dairy-free custard

Lunch boxes

Buying their lunch at school is not always an option and some children may prefer a lunch box. Aim to make the contents as varied as you can and pack them in a rigid insulated cool box to ensure they are as fresh as possible. Try the following dairy-free suggestions:
* Pita stuffed with chicken and salad, piece of fresh fruit, dairy-free calcium-enriched dessert, homemade oat bar or mini box of raisins, dairy-free drink
* Chicken drumsticks, pita bread, vegetable sticks, piece of fresh fruit, dairy-free yogurt (if this can be stored in a fridge until lunchtime), dairy-free muffin, dairy-free drink
* Salmon and vegetable wrap, piece of fresh fruit, homemade oat bar, dairy-free drink
* Couscous salad, piece of fresh fruit, dairy-free scone, orange juice
* Tuna, vegetable and rice salad, dried fruit, dairy-free dessert, carrot cake, dairy-free drink

It is important to go over the issues with your child's teacher but also to encourage children to manage their own allergies and intolerances, and to understand why swapping food with friends is not an option.

Afternoon tea and evening meal

Milky evening meals, which most children love, can all be made by directly substituting a dairy-free alternative for milk. These include many creamy pasta dishes, macaroni & cheese, crêpes, lasagnas, custards, and puddings. Many of these dishes can be made in bulk ahead of time and frozen. For plenty of inspiring evening-meal suggestions, look no further than the recipes in the second section of this book.
* Macaroni with Roast Cherry Tomatoes (see page 105)
* Carrot and Pumpkin Risotto (see page 98)
* Grilled Salmon Steaks with Creamy Lemon Sauce (see page 85)
* Fish Pie (see page 110)
* Pan-fried Chicken Breast with Creamy Basil Sauce (see page 88)

In addition, Mini C's Thai-style recipes bring lots of exciting new flavors and variety to the evening meal:
* Shredded Omelet in Mild Broth (see page 75)
* Steamed Cod Fillet with Triple-flavor Vegetables (see page 113)
* Steamed Chicken and Ginger Rice (see page 89)
* Yellow Curry with Lamb and Onions (see page 120)

Top tips for feeding babies and young children dairy-free

* Feed breast milk or the recommended infant formula for the first year.
* Weaning starts ideally at twelve months—but can start from six months. Suitable first foods include pureed potato, carrot, pear, apple (ripe banana and avocado not before six months).
* Avoid cow's milk until advised to reintroduce it by your health professional.
* Include foods rich in iron (e.g. red meat, egg yolk, green leafy vegetables, apricots, cereals) and vitamin C (e.g. citrus fruits, black currants, kiwi fruit, green leafy vegetables, broccoli, green peppers, and tomatoes) from six months.
* Avoid lowfat foods.
* Feed more varied meals by the end of the first year.
* By the age of one year, a child should be eating three family-type meals per day, plus snacks such as toast, dairy-free calcium-enriched yogurt, fruit, vegetable sticks, and fruit shakes—all according to individual appetite.
* Provide two to three servings of calcium-rich foods daily—see page 16.
* If children are away from home, make sure that their childcare givers understand the dairy-free diet.

eating out

When you are following a completely dairy-free diet, you cannot leave eating out to chance. Advance planning goes a long way. Think carefully about restaurants, and meals which friends and family might serve. In no time, questioning and sometimes bringing along dairy-free foods and drinks will become second nature. Always tell your host about your requirements—it saves embarrassing and awkward moments on the day. Catering processes can often limit the number of safe choices on the menu if you are worried about contamination and depending on how strict your diet is. Phoning ahead of time to discuss the menu options with the restaurant manager or chef can really help and you can then relax and enjoy your evening more. The following tips will help you.

Chinese

Chinese cooking is one of the best options for dairy-free eating out. This type of cooking traditionally uses very little dairy. Good choices include: lemon chicken, vegetable chow mein, crispy duck, sweet-and-sour chicken, and egg fried rice. Avoid the battered fruit and opt for fresh fruit such as the traditional lychees and sorbet (but beware of sherbets as some contain milk).

Thai

Akin to Chinese, Thai food includes virtually no dairy products in its savory dishes and very little in its desserts. Thai cooking tends to use coconut milk and cream in the same way as westerners use cow's milk and cream, so do be aware of the saturated fat content (see page 26 for more on this).

Mini C recommends the following options for eating out: glass noodle salad with ground pork and shrimp, green or red curry with beef and vegetables, stir-fried vegetables with garlic in mild broth, steamed or grilled sea bass with herbs, clear and mild cucumber soup with cilantro and, of course, plain boiled rice. It is traditional to share such a meal, which allows you to control your intake. Watch out for desserts made with cow's milk and condensed or evaporated milk.

Italian

Italian food provides one of the more challenging but certainly not impossible choices for a dairy-free meal out. Most of the pizzas, pastas, risottos, and lasagnas will be ruled out. Good choices include pasta with sun-dried tomato sauce (make sure butter is not used), focaccia and salads, or pizza with cheeseless toppings (choose your own at the restaurant). Alternatively some menus will provide a fresh fish and salad option. The breads being offered may be made with olive oil—ask the chef. Opt for fresh fruit desserts.

Indian

Traditionally ghee (clarified butter) is used for cooking Indian food. But in today's health-conscious environment, vegetable ghee or oil tends to be substituted. Many dishes use yogurt, and creamy dishes like korma will need to be avoided. Opt for vegetable curries made without yogurt or cream, rice and poppadams, and sorbet for dessert.

The steakouse

At the steakhouse, opt for the simple choices like grilled fish or lamb cutlets with baked potato. When requesting soup, ask for non-creamy options and always ask the manager/chef about the ingredients.

Burger bars

In burger bars, check that the bread is not made with butter or margarine and that the burger meat is not filled with any dairy source. Ask for a burger with a salad (check that the salad dressing is dairy-free) but no cheese. You can always bring your own dairy-free bun. Chicken pieces and drumsticks are an option if available. Many burger bars now have comprehensive ingredients lists for their products which you may find on their website or alternatively, ask the manager.

Going abroad

Order your dairy-free airline meal well in advance and find out what foods are available at your hotel and vacation destination. Consider taking some long-life dairy-free alternatives with you. It may also be worthwhile to learn how to ask for dairy-free options in the languages of the countries you are visiting or to have someone write this down on a piece of paper to show to the hotel or restaurant.

commonly asked questions

Do I need to take calcium supplements if I am on a dairy-free diet?
If dairy is being swapped for a calcium-enriched dairy alternative, it is highly unlikely. However, it will depend on how much you have a day, and the balance of calcium intake in the rest of your diet. Those on a completely dairy-free regime should see a registered nutritionist to check the nutrient content of their diet.

I am following a low-GI diet: do the milk alternatives have a higher GI?
Very often the dairy equivalents are similar to dairy in terms of GI (glycemic index) and also GL (glycemic load) but it is important to check with individual manufacturers.

Do I need to check out drugs and medicines if I am on a dairy-free diet?
More than 20 percent of prescription drugs and around 6 percent of over-the-counter medicines contain lactose.

Quantities are very small, so they should affect you only if you have a very severe allergy or lactose intolerance. However, to be on the safe side, always check with your doctor or pharmacist before taking anything. If you do react to a medicine, it may be the medicine rather then the lactose that you have reacted to.

How soon after starting a dairy-free diet will I feel a difference?
This varies. If you have symptoms relating to either a lactose intolerance or an allergy, you can feel the difference within days to weeks of being on a dairy-free diet.

Further help and information
Following a restricted diet of any type can be tricky, sometimes isolating, especially when it's long-term. Hearing about experiences from others can be a great support. There are a number of organizations which offer further information and support—see pages 140–141 for details.

from the chef

I found it very challenging to write the recipes for this book. Being Thai, I never really thought about dairy intolerances, simply because we hardly use dairy products in our cooking, if at all. So it was important for me find out more about lactose intolerance and how it affects people before I started writing the recipes.

When I researched the list of symptoms that can arise from consuming dairy products, one symptom really caught my eye and that was stomach pain. The description of the pain sounded so familiar and I suddenly thought to myself, perhaps I am actually one of those who suffers from this intolerance! I decided to test the theory by cutting out dairy products for two weeks just to see if my suspicion was right. To my great surprise, all the pain that I suffered totally vanished until I started adding milk to my tea and coffee and spreading butter on my toast again. I now use soy milk in my tea and cappuccino and substitute regular butter with vegan margarine whenever I can, although I do miss the real things from time to time. I have also learned a tremendous amount from Tanya Haffner, our nutritionist and dietitian. She guided me on ingredients and held me on a tight rein, making sure that I kept everything within healthy eating guidelines.

The recipes in this book are half Thai and half Western. The idea is that Eastern food is generally a healthy way of eating dairy-free, and many of the Thai recipes included have been adapted for the purposes of a healthy dairy-free diet—for example some of them use soy milk. The Western recipes provide dairy-free alternatives to dishes that traditionally contain cow's milk, such as ice cream, lasagna, and clam chowder.

Although I am Thai and specialize in Thai cooking, I am quite familiar with cooking Western dishes as I have spent a lot of time in the UK and US. Whatever you might think about Thai cooking, I can honestly tell you that Western cooking is just as confusing if you don't have a basic idea of the ingredients used. I had one of my chefs, Wimuta, from the Thai restaurant I used to run in London, as my assistant at the photo shoot. It was all going really well the first day when we did Thai dishes. However, when it came to making Western dishes, he was totally shocked and found the whole process very frustrating. He could not believe there were so many steps involved in making one simple dish like a fish pie, and told me that he'd rather cook the 180 Thai dishes available on our menu on a daily basis than have to make one of these Western recipes! But after a couple of days he became more familiar with the ingredients and from then on started to understand the process of Western cooking.

Therefore, regardless of how well you think you can cook, it is vital to understand your ingredients before you can develop your creativity. Like me, you will find that using soy alternatives in recipes is surprisingly easy to do, and the results are delicious. We can all learn, be it fast or slow, and you will get there in the end... so let me guide you.

1

breakfasts and
late-night dishes

luxury breakfast muesli

Store-bought muesli can be luxurious with just a few additions. You can prepare it in advance, but make sure you keep the toasted muesli and dried fruits separately in airtight containers in a cool, dry place. Just keep the soy milk within reach!

2oz (about ⅓–½ cup) mixed nuts and seeds, such as slivered almonds, chopped hazelnuts, and sunflower seeds
1¼ cups unsweetened dairy-free muesli
3½ oz (about ¾ cup) mixed dried fruit, such as sun-dried small bananas, raisins and golden raisins, dates, apricots and prunes, seeded and chopped

For serving
5–7 cups soy milk
Fresh peach and strawberry slices
Brown sugar or honey (optional)

Serves 4

Toast the mixed nuts and seeds in a dry frying pan (do not use any oil) over a low heat until golden, tossing and turning them frequently to avoid burning. Remove from the pan and let cool; do not cover.

Toast the muesli in the same way and let cool.

Mix the dried fruit with the cooled nuts, seeds, and muesli.

Serve the muesli with soy milk and, if you wish, some fresh peach and strawberry slices, and a sprinkling of brown sugar or a drizzle of honey.

PER SERVING: 256 CALORIES, 9.1G FAT, 1.3G SATURATED FAT, 15.4G TOTAL PROTEIN, 8.8G SOY PROTEIN, 360MG CALCIUM, 50MG SODIUM

coconut crêpes with banana and maple syrup

Being Thai, I find it hard to get away from coconut whether that be coconut milk, juice, or dried coconut. It is one of the main ingredients in our cooking, so here it is—enjoy my kind of crêpes.

3½ tablespoons sugar
4½ tablespoons rice flour
⅔ cup all-purpose flour, sifted
⅔ cup plus 1 tablespoon dried coconut
1 large egg
1¼ cups soy milk
3–4 dried figs, finely chopped
1 teaspoon grated lime zest
A little vegan margarine or vegetable oil, for frying

For the maple syrup banana slices
1 tablespoon vegan margarine
2 bananas, peeled and cut into ¼-inch slices
2 tablespoons maple syrup
1½ tablespoons freshly squeezed lime juice

For serving
Lime wedges
Maple syrup

Serves 4

First make the maple syrup banana slices. In a frying pan, melt the margarine over a low heat and add the bananas. Gently stir until the slices are well coated. Add the maple syrup and lime juice and gently mix in. Remove from the heat and set aside.

Put the sugar, rice flour, regular flour, and dried coconut in a large bowl and stir to mix well. In a separate bowl, beat the egg and soy milk together using a fork. Pour the egg mixture into the bowl of dry ingredients and gently incorporate, then whisk to form a batter, making sure there are no big lumps. Stir in the chopped figs and lime zest.

Heat a small amount of the margarine or oil in a nonstick frying pan. Pour in about 3 tablespoons of the batter and quickly spread to a thin layer with the back of a spoon to keep an even thickness. Cook the crêpe for about 40–50 seconds over a high heat until bubbles appear on the surface, then gently turn it over with a spatula and cook the other side until golden. Use the rest of the mixture to make more crêpes. Serve the crêpes with the maple syrup banana slices, lime wedges for squeezing, and more maple syrup for drizzling.

PER SERVING: 489 CALORIES, 21.4G FAT, 10.1G SATURATED FAT, 8.7G TOTAL PROTEIN, 2.3G SOY PROTEIN, 104MG CALCIUM, 150MG SODIUM

warm sweet potatoes in ginger syrup

This is my most favorite sweet dish—it is very soothing. It is enjoyed by Thais as a snack at any time of day, and as it uses no dairy products, I thoroughly recommend it to everyone on a dairy-free diet.

2½ cups water
18oz sweet potatoes, peeled and cut into
  pieces about ¾ x ⅜ inch
½ cup sugar
1 large piece of ginger, washed, cut into pieces,
  and lightly pounded

Serves 4

Bring the water to a boil in a pan and add the sweet potatoes. Once the water returns to a boil, add the ginger and continue to simmer for about 20 minutes until the potato pieces are tender and cooked through.

Add the sugar and stir gently until it is thoroughly dissolved.

Remove the pan from the heat and transfer the sweet potatoes into individual serving bowls, discarding the ginger pieces.

PER SERVING: 210 CALORIES, 0.4G FAT, 0.2G SATURATED FAT, 1.6G TOTAL PROTEIN, 33MG CALCIUM, 50MG SODIUM

oatmeal with honey

Here is a healthy, dairy-free, and delicious way of making my favorite oatmeal. You can sweeten it to your own taste with a dash of honey or a sprinkling of brown sugar. It is also good with raisins.

1½ cups rolled oats
3 cups soy milk
3 cups water
Honey or brown sugar (optional)
Raisins (optional)

Serves 4

Mix the oats, soy milk, and water thoroughly in a sucepan.

Bring the mixture to a boil over medium heat, then lower the heat and continue to simmer for about 5 minutes, until the oatmeal thickens, stirring occasionally to prevent it sticking to the bottom of the pan.

Serve sweetened with honey or brown sugar and a sprinkling of raisins, if you wish.

PER SERVING: 187 CALORIES, 5.4G FAT, 0.8G SATURATED FAT, 10.5G TOTAL PROTEIN, 5G SOYA PROTEIN, 43MG CALCIUM, 50MG SODIUM

warm prunes with coconut and orange zest

french toast drizzled with honey

When we think of prunes, we think of a healthy breakfast or dessert, don't we? This dish makes a light but warm breakfast on a freezing morning. It is also a natural way to ease a constipation problem, if you have one.

French toast is very popular among upper-class Thais and I must say it is yummy, although unlike American French toast, the Thai version is deep fried. It tastes and smells like a doughnut but with an alluring fragrance of honey.

9oz pitted dried prunes
1 cup pure orange juice
1 large orange
2 tablespoons coconut cream
Soft brown sugar, for sprinkling

Serves 4

Vegetable oil, for deep-frying
4 medium eggs
4 medium slices of white bread
¼ cup honey

Serves 4

Place the prunes and orange juice in a pan and leave to soak for 30 minutes. Bring to a boil, then reduce the heat, cover, and cook for approximately 20 minutes.

Meanwhile, thinly peel the zest (the orange-colored part of the rind only) from the orange and cut it into fine shreds—you will need 2 tablespoons.

Spoon the cooked prunes into individual bowls, add ½ tablespoon of the coconut cream to each one and sprinkle with the orange zest and soft brown sugar to serve.

PER SERVING: 175 CALORIES, 2.6G FAT, 2.2G SATURATED FAT, 2.7G TOTAL PROTEIN, 55MG CALCIUM, 10MG SODIUM

Heat enough oil to cover a slice of bread in a deep, wide frying pan over medium heat until the temperature reaches about 350°F. If the oil is not hot enough before you add the bread, you will end up with very oily toasts.

Meanwhile, in a large bowl, beat the eggs with a fork until they have a runny texture.

Dip one slice of bread at a time into the eggs and coat it well, then gently place it in the frying pan, making sure it is covered with oil. Flip the bread over with tongs and continue to turn it backwards and forwards until it is golden brown. Deep-fry the remaining bread slices in the same way.

Remove the toasts from the pan with the tongs and drain them well on layers of folded paper towels.

Drizzle the toasts with honey and serve.

PER SERVING: 246 CALORIES, 11.3G FAT, 2.2G SATURATED FAT, 9.2G TOTAL PROTEIN, 68MG CALCIUM, 250MG SODIUM

fried rice with ham and peas topped with poached egg

Typical Thai—rice for breakfast, lunch, dinner, and even for a late-night snack. We can't get enough of it. The Thais treat rice in the same way as people in the West treat their bread and potatoes.

1¾ cups vegetable or peanut oil
11oz boneless skinless chicken,
    thinly sliced along the grain
11oz sliced cooked ham, cut into small square pieces
2¼ lb boiled rice (see right)
3oz (scant cup) onion, thinly sliced
3oz (about ½–⅔ cup) peas (shelled weight)
1 teaspoon sugar
2 teaspoons salt
2 tablespoons tomato ketchup
4 eggs

Serves 4

Heat a wok or frying pan over medium heat, then add the oil and heat. Add the pieces of chicken and stir around until almost cooked, then add the ham and gently stir with the chicken for 30 seconds.

Add the boiled rice and toss and turn together with the ham and chicken pieces, then add the onion and peas. Stir the vegetables into the rice.

Season with the sugar, salt, and tomato ketchup, stirring to make sure that the color from the ketchup is evenly distributed.

Meanwhile, bring some water to a boil in a saucepan. Break the eggs, one by one, into a saucer and slip them into the water. Turn off the heat and cover the pan. Let them poach for 3 minutes until the whites are set but the yolks are still runny. Serve the fried rice with the eggs on top.

PER SERVING: 619 CALORIES, 32.9G FAT, 5.5G SATURATED FAT, 38.5G TOTAL PROTEIN, 53MG CALCIUM, 1,480MG SODIUM

boiled rice

Here are two ways of cooking rice: using an electric rice cooker or in a saucepan on top of the stove. In Thai cooking we do not season the rice with oil or salt.

14oz (about 2 cups) jasmine fragrant rice or plain long-grain rice
2¾ cups water

Makes 2¼ lb
Serves 4

Using an electric rice cooker
Put the rice in a fine mesh strainer and rinse it under warm running water until the water runs clear.

Place the rice in the pot that comes with the electric rice cooker and add the measured water.

Wipe any excess water from the outside of the pot, then place it back in the cooker and let it cook until the light switches off automatically.

Let stand for another 10 minutes before serving the rice or using it in a recipe.

Using a pan
Rinse the rice well as described above, then put it in a saucepan with the measured water.

Place the pan over a medium-low heat and bring to a boil leaving the lid on. Stir the rice gently from time to time—take care not to break the grains. Once the water has begun to evaporate, turn the heat to very low and continue to simmer with the lid on.

When the water has completely evaporated and the rice is cooked, turn off the heat. Let the pan stand, covered, for another 10 minutes before serving the rice or using it in a recipe.

PER SERVING: 330 CALORIES, 0.8G FAT, 0.2G SATURATED FAT, 7.7G TOTAL PROTEIN, 4MG CALCIUM, 10MG SODIUM

rice soup with red snapper and cilantro root

Cilantro roots have an intense flavor and are widely used in Thai cooking. You can buy cilantro with its roots still attached from Asian food stores. If unavailable, use the stalks of the herb instead.

7½ cups vegetable broth
3 fresh cilantro roots, crushed
14oz (about 3–4 cups) boiled rice (see page 49)
2 tablespoons Thai fish sauce
2 teaspoons sugar
1lb red snapper fillets
Salt and ground white pepper

For the chilies in vinegar
4 large mixed chilies, sliced into thin rings
Distilled malt vinegar

For the crispy garlic
3 tablespoons vegetable oil
6 garlic cloves, crushed

For the garnish
2 scallions, chopped
Handful of cilantro sprigs

Serves 4

First prepare the chilies in vinegar. Put the sliced chilies in a bowl and pour in enough vinegar to cover them completely. Let soak for a minimum of 30 minutes.

To make the crispy garlic, put the oil and crushed garlic in a frying pan or wok over a low heat and keep stirring until the garlic turns golden, but not burnt. Transfer into a bowl and set aside.

Pour the broth into a large pot, add the crushed cilantro roots and bring to a boil. Add the cooked rice and simmer for 15 minutes. Season with the fish sauce and sugar, then add the fish fillets and simmer until the fish is cooked.

Transfer the rice soup into individual serving bowls, season with salt and pepper to taste, and stir well. Garnish each bowl with the crispy garlic, scallions and cilantro sprigs, and serve with the chilies in vinegar on the side.

PER SERVING: 338 CALORIES, 10.3G FAT, 1.3G SATURATED FAT, 28.2G TOTAL PROTEIN, 118MG CALCIUM, 1,340MG SODIUM

2

salads and
appetizers

savory assorted fruit salad with crispy shallots and rice crackers

This is a very popular dish in Thailand. It's an all year-round dish for the Thais as our climate is almost always on the warm side.

½ handful of seedless grapes
1 Granny Smith apple, cored and chopped into small cubes
1 red apple, cored and chopped into small cubes
1 firm ripe papaya, peeled and chopped into small cubes
A few cilantro leaves, for garnishing
Rice crackers, for serving

For the dressing
1 tablespoon Thai fish sauce
1 Thai chili, finely chopped
1 garlic clove, crushed
1 teaspoon sugar
3 tablespoons shredded carrot
1½ tablespoons freshly squeezed lemon juice

For the crispy shallots
2 tablespoons vegetable oil
2 shallots, thinly sliced

Serves 2

First make the crispy shallots. Heat the oil in a wok over medium heat. Add the shallot slices and deep-fry, stirring, until they turn golden brown and crisp. Remove from the hot oil and drain well on layers of paper towel. Let cool.

Make the dressing by combining the fish sauce, chili, garlic, and sugar in a bowl and stirring until the sugar dissolves. Add the carrot and lemon juice and mix well.

Put all the fruit in a large bowl, add the dressing, and gently toss and turn. Add the crispy shallots and toss together one more time. Transfer to a large plate, sprinkle with cilantro leaves, and serve with rice crackers on the side.

PER SERVING: 249 CALORIES, 11.4G FAT, 1.3G SATURATED FAT, 2.8G TOTAL PROTEIN, 56MG CALCIUM, 590MG SODIUM

cold wild rice salad with herbs

Rice is not usually eaten cold in Thailand, but I like it as long as it is served as a salad, such as this one. This recipe couldn't be simpler, it really is just a question of throwing ingredients together. Great for a packed lunch.

7oz (about 1½–2 cups) hot cooked wild rice
Salt, to taste
1 tomato, chopped
3 tablespoons canned kidney beans, drained and rinsed
2 tablespoons chopped red pepper
2 tablespoons chopped green pepper
1 tablespoon chopped basil leaves
1 garlic clove, crushed
1 teaspoon grated lime zest
1 tablespoon freshly squeezed lime juice
2 tablespoons freshly squeezed orange juice
Crispy shallots (see left)

Serves 2

Place the hot wild rice in a bowl and stir in salt to taste. Let cool.

Add all the remaining ingredients to the cooled rice and gently mix together well.

PER SERVING: 260 CALORIES, 11.7G FAT, 1.4G SATURATED FAT, 7.4G TOTAL PROTEIN, 39MG CALCIUM, 190MG SODIUM

spinach and tomato quiche

This is the dish I make to entertain friends on a very casual day. It is one step up from a pizza, requiring slightly more preparation and effort, so your friends should feel a little more valued than if you were to serve them with a plain pizza.

1¾ cups all-purpose flour, plus extra for dusting
½ cup plus 1 tablespoon chilled vegan margarine, cut into small cubes
Salt and ground black pepper
3½ tablespoons cold water
2 eggs and 2 egg yolks
2 cups minus 2 tablespoons soy cream
1 cup grated cheddar-style soy cheese
1 zucchini, thinly sliced
2 handfuls of spinach leaves, blanched, drained, and excess water squeezed out
2 tomatoes, thinly sliced

Serves 6–8

Preheat the oven to 350ºF.

Place the flour, vegan margarine, and half a teaspoon salt in a food processor and whizz until the mixture forms into crumbs. Add the water and whizz briefly again until a firm dough is formed. (You can also do this by hand.)

Roll out the dough on a floured counter and use it to line a 9-inch removable-bottomed quiche pan. Press the dough well into the sides of the pan and trim away any excess hanging over the edge. Prick the bottom of the pie shell with a fork, then fill with crumpled foil.

Bake in the oven for 15 minutes or until the crust is cooked through. Take the pie shell out of the oven and remove the crumpled foil. Lower the oven temperature to 325ºF.

Make the filling for the quiche by beating together the eggs and egg yolks and soy cream, until well blended. Stir in the grated cheese and all the prepared vegetables, then season with salt and pepper to taste.

Pour the filling into the pie shell and bake in the oven for 25–30 minutes until the filling is set and the surface is slightly brown.

Serve warm or cold with salad.

PER SERVING (FOR 8): 402 CALORIES, 30.1G FAT, 5.6G SATURATED FAT, 10.2 TOTAL PROTEIN, 2.2G SOY PROTEIN, 190MG CALCIUM, 350MG SODIUM

crispy vegetables with plum sauce

A healthier and dairy-free alternative to the usual battered foods. You can use any of your favorite vegetables, provided they are firm and solid in texture. For the plum sauce, you can buy jars of salted plums in most Asian supermarkets.

1¾ cups all-purpose flour
1¼ cups water
½ teaspoon salt
1 teaspoon ground white pepper
Vegetable oil, for deep-frying
2½ oz baby corn, trimmed
1½ cups broccoli florets, cut into bite-size pieces
3oz carrots, cut into sticks about
   1½ inches long and ⅜ inch thick
1½ cups cauliflower florets, cut into bite-size pieces
1½ cups green beans, trimmed
1 large onion, cut into 8 sections

For the plum sauce
1 salted plum, pitted and mashed
¾ cup distilled malt vinegar
½ cup sugar
½ cup water
1 tablespoon shredded carrot

Serves 4

First make the plum sauce. Place the salted plum, vinegar, sugar, and water in a small saucepan over a low heat and stir until the sugar dissolves. Add the shredded carrot and simmer, stirring, until the sauce thickens. Remove from the heat and let cool. You can make this sauce weeks in advance, provided you keep it covered in the fridge, but be sure to return it to room temperature before using it so it isn't too sticky.

Put the flour in a large bowl, stir in the water, and whisk to make a smooth paste. Add the salt and white pepper and give it a good whisk until the salt has dissolved.

Heat enough oil for deep-frying in a wok over a high heat until it reaches 350°F.

Dip each type of vegetable individually into the bowl of flour paste, then gently lift out a few pieces at a time and let the excess paste drip off.

Deep-fry the coated vegetables in batches in the hot oil until golden brown all over. Remove them from the wok using a wire spoon or tongs, drain them well on layers of paper towels and keep them warm. Repeat until all the vegetables are cooked.

Serve the crispy vegetables with the plum sauce on the side.

PER SERVING: 581 CALORIES, 26.5G FAT, 3.1G SATURATED FAT, 9.1G TOTAL PROTEIN, 135MG CALCIUM, 460MG SODIUM

cashew salad with ginger and chilies

In Thailand, instead of having roasted peanuts with a cold beer in a pub, we tend to order more substantial snacks. This is a good example of how to convert plain cashews into something more daring.

1⅓ cups raw cashews
1 thumb-size piece of fresh ginger,
   peeled and cut into matchsticks
2 Thai chilies, finely chopped
3 scallions, sliced into thin rings
A few grinds of sea salt (or kosher salt)

Serves 2–3

Preheat the oven to 325°F and dry-roast the cashews for 5–10 minutes.

While the cashews are still hot, place in a large bowl with the ginger, chilies, and scallions. Gently mix, then season with salt to taste and serve.

PER SERVING (FOR 3): 321 CALORIES, 27.5G FAT, 3G SATURATED FAT, 9.1G TOTAL PROTEIN, 20MG CALCIUM, 210MG SODIUM

smoked salmon (lox) spicy salad

This is a lovely and fragrant salad which looks very colorful on the plate. It's a different way of serving smoked salmon—the dressing is quite refreshing with a bit of a kick from the chilies. Again, the ingredients are readily available.

2 Thai chilies
2 garlic cloves
2 tablespoons lime juice
1 teaspoon sugar
7oz (about 1 cup) smoked salmon slices
4 shallots, thinly sliced
1-inch piece of fresh ginger,
   peeled and cut into matchsticks
A few chives, cut into 2-inch lengths, for garnishing

Serves 2

Make a dressing by lightly crushing together the chilies and garlic cloves using a mortar and pestle. Add the lime juice and sugar and stir well to combine.

Put the smoked salmon in a large bowl, add the shallots and ginger, then pour the dressing over it. Transfer to a large serving plate and garnish with chives.

PER SERVING: 166 CALORIES, 4.6G FAT, 0.9G SATURATED FAT, 26.4G TOTAL PROTEIN, 29MG CALCIUM, 1,880MG SODIUM

grilled spiced scallops

This is my healthier version of Thai fast food, inspired by the charcoal-grilled fish and pork balls sold on the streets all over Thailand. The sauce can be refrigerated for up to 3 months.

2 garlic cloves, pounded with
  1 fresh cilantro root to make
  a paste
⅓ cup coconut cream
1½ tablespoons Thai fish sauce
½ teaspoon ground cumin
½ teaspoon ground coriander
½ teaspoon white pepper
18oz shelled scallops
2 large red peppers, seeded,
  cut into 1-inch squares

A few cilantro leaves, for
  garnishing

For the sweet chili and garlic sauce
6 fresh red chilies
6 garlic cloves
¾ cup distilled malt vinegar
½ cup sugar
1 teaspoon salt

Serves 4

First make the sweet chili and garlic sauce. Seed 3 of the chilies and chop all 6 of them. Whizz the chillies and garlic in a small food processor, or pound them using a mortar and pestle, to form a paste. Heat the vinegar in a small pan over a low heat and stir in the sugar and salt until dissolved. Add the chili and garlic paste and simmer, stirring occasionally, until the sauce thickens. Set aside to cool.

Combine the garlic and cilantro paste with the coconut cream and fish sauce in a large bowl. Gently stir in the cumin, ground coriander, and white pepper until well blended. Add the scallops to the paste, stirring to coat them, then cover and place in the fridge to marinate for about 20 minutes.

Soak 8–10 wooden skewers, 7 inches long, in cold water. Preheat the broiler to high. Thread 3–4 scallops onto each skewer, alternating with pieces of red pepper. Broil the skewers for about 2 minutes, turning halfway through cooking, until the scallops are opaque. Serve hot, drizzled with the sweet chili and garlic sauce and garnished with cilantro leaves.

PER SERVING: 351 CALORIES, 10.8G FAT, 7.8G SATURATED FAT, 27.2G TOTAL PROTEIN, 154MG CALCIUM, 920MG SODIUM

aromatic seared tuna steak and citrus salsa

The Thais love to mix savory ingredients with fruit. We even dip our fruit in spicy salt and sugar! This is a lovely, refreshing dish which is so light yet packed full of flavors.

2 garlic cloves, finely chopped
1 teaspoon ground coriander
1 teaspoon salt
2 teaspoons freshly squeezed
  lime juice
4 tuna steaks
1 tablespoon olive oil
4 cilantro sprigs, for garnishing

For the citrus salsa
1 small orange or mandarin,
  peeled, membranes removed
  from each segment and cut
  into small pieces

½ grapefruit, prepared in the
  same way as the orange
Juice of 1 lemon
A few fresh pineapple slices,
  cut into small pieces
1 tomato, chopped
2 tablespoons chopped
  shallots
1 tablespoon Thai fish sauce
1 Thai chili, crushed

Serves 4

Make a marinade by mixing the garlic, ground coriander, salt, and lime juice in a large bowl. Add the tuna steaks one by one, turning them to make sure they are well coated with the mixture. Cover the bowl with plastic wrap and let marinate in the fridge for about 30 minutes.

Prepare the citrus salsa while waiting for the fish to marinate. Mix all the salsa ingredients together well, cover, and chill until needed.

Heat a grill pan over a high heat and brush with the oil. Brush the tuna steaks on both sides with any remaining marinade and grill for 2–3 minutes on each side.

Carefully cut each tuna steak into thin slices, garnish with the cilantro sprigs and serve with the citrus salsa.

PER SERVING: 261 CALORIES, 9.8G FAT, 2.7G SATURATED FAT, 37.1G TOTAL PROTEIN, 52MG CALCIUM, 850MG SODIUM

peanut-crusted black tiger shrimp on shredded rutabaga and carrot salad

I thought it would be interesting to have the crunchy texture of peanuts married closely with shrimp, as they go so well together. See what you think.

1 garlic clove, pounded with
   1 fresh cilantro root to make a paste
1½ tablespoons Thai fish sauce
About ⅓ cup water
1 egg, beaten
⅔ cup rice flour
¼ cup cornstarch
2 kaffir lime leaves, finely shredded
½ teaspoon white pepper
Vegetable oil, for deep-frying
16 medium raw black tiger shrimp, peeled and
   deveined but with the tails left on
⅔ cup dry-roasted peanuts, coarsely chopped
4 cilantro sprigs, for garnishing

For the rutabaga and carrot salad
1 teaspoon sugar
1 Thai chili, crushed
1 tablespoon Thai fish sauce
1½ tablespoons freshly squeezed lemon juice
1½ oz (about ¼–⅔ cup) rutabaga, cut into matchsticks
1½ oz (about ¼–⅔ cup) carrot, cut into matchsticks
1 large tomato, cut into wedges

Serves 4

Make the salad by mixing together the sugar, chili, fish sauce, and lemon juice in a bowl to make a dressing. Then add the rutabaga, carrot, and tomato, and gently toss and turn until they are all well coated in the dressing.

Mix the garlic and cilantro paste with the fish sauce in a bowl. Whisk in the water and beaten egg.

Combine the rice flour, cornstarch, kaffir lime leaves, and pepper in a separate bowl and slowly add the garlic and cilantro mixture, and some more water if needed, to make a thick batter.

Heat enough oil for deep-frying in a wok over a high heat until it reaches 350°F. Holding each shrimp by the tail, dip it in the batter, then coat it with the peanuts by using your other hand to sprinkle the peanuts all over it.

Slip the shrimp carefully into the hot oil, 4 or 5 at a time, and fry until crisp and golden. Lift them out of the wok, drain them on layers of paper towels and keep them warm while you cook the rest.

Arrange the rutabaga and carrot salad on individual serving plates, place 4 of the crispy shrimp on top of each portion, and garnish with a cilantro sprig.

PER SERVING: 438 CALORIES, 27.4G FAT, 4.1G SATURATED FAT, 21.1G TOTAL PROTEIN, 95MG CALCIUM, 1,300MG SODIUM

scented broiled fish salad

A very light and aromatic dish, full of flavor and fragrance. The cilantro root and garlic paste really does make a difference to the taste of this monkfish salad and no doubt the dish would have been very bland without it.

2 garlic cloves, pounded with
   1 fresh cilantro root to make a paste
⅓ cup coconut cream
1 tablespoon Thai fish sauce
½ teaspoon ground cumin
Ground black pepper
14oz monkfish fillet, cut into 12 cubes
½ red pepper, seeded and cut into bite-sized pieces

For serving
2 tablespoons sweet chili and garlic sauce
   (see page 60, or use ready-made)
Mixed herb salad
1 lime

Serves 2

Combine the garlic and cilantro paste with the coconut cream and fish sauce in a large bowl. Gently stir in the cumin and black pepper until well blended. Add the monkfish pieces, stirring to coat them, then cover and place in the fridge to marinate for about 20 minutes.

Soak 4 bamboo skewers, 7 inches long, in cold water.

When you are ready to cook, preheat the broiler to high. Thread 3 pieces of monkfish onto each skewer, alternating with pieces of red pepper. Broil for about 2 minutes, turning half-way through, until the fish is cooked.

Serve hot, drizzled with sweet chili and garlic sauce on a bed of mixed herb salad with a squeeze of lime juice.

PER SERVING: 169 CALORIES, 9.3G FAT, 7.6G SATURATED FAT, 17.7G TOTAL PROTEIN, 22MG CALCIUM, 310MG SODIUM

spicy smoked mackerel dip

At my restaurant, we used a mortar and pestle to blend ingredients, which gives much greater control over the final texture. However, most households in the West are more likely to have a food processor, so that is what I have used here.

6 garlic cloves
1 red onion, cut in half
4oz whole red and green chilies
½ a red pepper and ½ a green pepper, seeded
4 tablespoons Thai fish sauce
½ tablespoon sugar
¼ cup freshly squeezed lemon juice
2 tablespoons water, boiled and cooled
6oz smoked mackerel fillets, broken into small pieces
Chopped cilantro leaves, to taste
Toasted bruschetta or fresh raw vegetables (such as carrots,
   celery, cucumber, tomatoes, and zucchini), for serving

Serves 3–4

Preheat the oven to 300°F. Place the garlic, red onion, chilies, and pepper halves on a baking tray and bake in the oven for about 45 minutes or until they are tender, turning once. Remove them from the oven and let cool a little.

Peel the skins off the chilies and peppers, and cut the onion and peppers into small cubes.

Put the garlic and onion into the food processor first, and gently blend to make a coarse paste. Add the chilies, peppers, fish sauce, sugar, lemon juice, and water, followed by the fish pieces, and blend to make a coarse paste.

Transfer the paste to a bowl and gently fold in the chopped cilantro leaves to taste. This is great served with toasted bruschetta and also as a dip with fresh raw vegetables.

PER SERVING (FOR 3): 266 CALORIES, 18.5G FAT, 4.5G SATURATED FAT, 16.2G TOTAL PROTEIN, 51MG CALCIUM, 1,980MG SODIUM

curried fishcakes

If you can't find grey feather fish paste in your local Asian supermarkets, and if cost is no object, then use monkfish instead. The texture of the finished fishcakes must be quite bouncy so a fish like cod would not really be suitable.

1½ tablespoons vegetable oil, plus extra for deep-frying
10 kaffir lime leaves, finely chopped
¼ cup ready-made Thai red curry paste
18oz pack grey feather fish paste, or monkfish fillet
1 egg
4 teaspoons sugar
2 tablespoons Thai fish sauce
Handful of green beans, trimmed and finely chopped
Handful of sweet basil leaves, chopped (optional)

For the chili and peanut dip
Scant cup sweet chilli and garlic sauce
  (see page 60, or use ready-made)
⅝–inch slice cucumber, quartered, seeded
  and then finely chopped
¼ cup carrot, finely chopped
1½ tablespoons roasted peanuts, crushed
1 tablespoon distilled malt vinegar

Makes 20 bite-size cakes (serves 4–5)

First heat the measured oil in a wok or a saucepan and stir-fry half of the kaffir lime leaves with the red curry paste for about a minute, taking care not to burn the curry paste.

Make the chili and peanut dip. Put all the ingredients in a bowl and stir together until blended, then set aside to cool.

To make the fishcakes, put the fish paste or monkfish, red curry paste, egg, sugar, and fish sauce in a food processor and blend until a thick paste forms, ensuring that the texture of the fish is chewy.

Transfer the paste to a large bowl and knead with your hands. Add the green beans, sweet basil leaves (if using), and the remaining kaffir lime leaves, and continue to knead until all the ingredients are well distributed.

Lightly oil your fingertips, take 1 tablespoon of paste and roll it into a ball, then flatten it slightly by pressing. Continue in this way until all the mixture is used.

Heat enough oil for deep-frying in a wok over a high heat until it reaches 350°F.

Working in batches, fry the fishcakes, turning them often, until they are golden brown all over and float to the surface. Use a slotted spoon to remove them from the hot oil, drain them well on paper towels and keep them warm. Continue until all the cakes are fried.

Serve the fishcakes with the chili and peanut dip.

PER SERVING (FOR 4): 429 CALORIES, 23.1G FAT, 2.9G SATURATED FAT, 25.6G TOTAL PROTEIN, 64MG CALCIUM, 240MG SODIUM

crispy shrimp crêpes with cucumber relish

So fragile and delicious—please handle these with care once they are cooked. They taste like shrimp chips but with real shrimp inside.

14oz raw shrimp, peeled
and deveined
1 egg, beaten
1 tablespoon Thai fish sauce
Pinch of ground white pepper
1 garlic clove, pounded with
½ fresh cilantro root to
make a paste
8 large spring-roll wrappers,
about 10 inches square
Vegetable oil, for deep-frying

For the cucumber relish
1 cup distilled malt vinegar
½ cup water
3 tablespoons sugar
1 teaspoon salt
½ medium cucumber,
quartered lengthways,
seeded, and finely sliced
4 shallots, thinly sliced
2 fresh red chilies, finely sliced

Serves 4

First make the cucumber relish. Heat the vinegar and water in a small saucepan over a low heat. Add the sugar and salt and stir until dissolved. Remove from the heat and set aside to cool, then stir in the cucumbers, shallots, and chilies.

Put the shrimp into a food processor and whizz to make a thick paste. Transfer the paste to a bowl and stir in the beaten egg. Add the fish sauce, white pepper, and garlic and cilantro paste and mix together with your hands, pressing and turning. Divide the shrimp paste between 4 of the spring-roll sheets, spreading it thinly over the whole surface. Top each one with another sheet and use a rolling pin to seal the sheets together. Cut each large shrimp crêpe into 4 equal square pieces, making a total of 16 smaller crêpes, sealing each one as before.

Heat enough oil for deep-frying in a pan over a high heat to about 350°F. Lower a few crêpes at a time gently into the oil and keep turning them until golden brown all over. Use a pair of tongs or a slotted spoon to remove them from the wok and drain on paper towels. Keep warm while you fry the rest. Serve with the cucumber relish.

PER SERVING: 505 CALORIES, 23G FAT, 2.9G SATURATED FAT, 26.8G TOTAL PROTEIN, 134MG CALCIUM, 1,360MG SODIUM

caesar salad with chicken

If you love Caesar salad, why not try this dairy-free version? Please note that children, pregnant women, and the elderly should not eat undercooked eggs.

2 tablespoons olive oil
4 thick slices of day-old bread,
cut into ⅜-inch cubes
1 romaine lettuce
¼ cup vegan Parmesan-style
cheese, finely pared into
shavings, or grated

For the dressing
⅓ cup olive oil
4 garlic cloves

2 anchovy fillets in oil, drained
and chopped
1 tablespoon balsamic vinegar
5 teaspoons Dijon mustard
1 egg

For the chicken
1 tablespoon olive oil
Sea salt (or kosher salt)
and black pepper
2 skinless boneless chicken
breasts

Serves 4

Preheat the oven to 425°F. Put the oil in a bowl, add the bread cubes, and toss to coat in the oil. Place the bread cubes on a baking sheet and bake in the oven for 6 minutes or until crisp and golden. Set aside.

Reduce the oven temperature to 350°F to cook the chicken. Mix the olive oil with salt and pepper, to taste, and rub all over the chicken. Cook in the oven for about 20 minutes or until cooked through. Slice and keep warm.

Meanwhile, make the dressing. Put the oil in a small saucepan, add the whole garlic cloves and the anchovies and heat gently for 5 minutes until the garlic is soft and golden. Let cool, then strain the oil and reserve. Mash the garlic and anchovies to a paste and mix in the vinegar and mustard. Gradually whisk in the strained oil in a steady stream until the mixture thickens.

Cook the egg in boiling water for only 2 minutes, then cool it under cold running water. Shell the egg and whisk only the yolk directly into the dressing until evenly combined. Tear the lettuce leaves into a large salad bowl. Scatter the croûtons and cheese shavings over it, pour in the dressing and toss well. Arrange the warm sliced chicken on top and serve.

PER SERVING: 455 CALORIES, 28.3G FAT, 5.2G SATURATED FAT, 26.6G TOTAL PROTEIN, 151MG CALCIUM, 680MG SODIUM

thai broiled beef salad

This is very Thai. It is another way of making beef more interesting, apart from the usual stir-frying and stewing methods. Although quite a filling dish, it is great for your waistline as long as you trim any fat from the beef. Especially great with an ice-cold beer!

Vegetable oil or butter, for greasing
14oz beef rump, in one piece
2 Thai chilies
2 garlic cloves, roughly chopped
3 tablespoons Thai fish sauce
4½ tablespoons freshly squeezed lemon juice
½ tablespoon sugar
⅔ cup cucumber, finely sliced
2 tomatoes, cut into wedges
½ onion, thinly sliced
2 scallions, chopped
½ handful of cilantro leaves, for garnishing

Serves 2

Preheat the broiler to medium-high and lightly grease the broiler rack.

Place the beef on the rack and broil for 2–3 minutes on each side until it is medium-rare, then set aside to cool.

Pound the chilies and garlic together into a paste using a mortar and pestle. Transfer to a large bowl and stir in the fish sauce, lemon juice, and sugar.

Thinly slice the beef and add it to the bowl, along with the cucumber, tomatoes, onion, and scallions and very gently toss together.

Transfer the salad to serving bowls and garnish with the cilantro leaves.

PER SERVING: 375 CALORIES, 16G FAT, 6.9G SATURATED FAT, 45.7G TOTAL PROTEIN, 54MG CALCIUM, 1,830MG SODIUM

spicy chilled cucumber and ham salad

This salad, with an oil-free dressing, is so simple to make and the ingredients are pretty common and easily found, especially in your own fridge. It's important to use good-quality ham.

7oz (about 1⅔ cups) cooked sliced ham, cut into long thin strips
1 large cucumber, cut in half lengthways,
    seeded, and sliced
½ onion, thinly sliced into rings
A few cilantro sprigs, for garnishing

For the dressing
2 garlic cloves, crushed
2 Thai chilies, lightly crushed
½ tablespoon sugar
¼ cup Thai fish sauce
⅓ cup plus 1 tablespoon freshly squeezed lemon juice

Serves 2

Make the dressing by combining the garlic, chilies, sugar, fish sauce, and lemon juice in a bowl. Mix well and set aside.

Place the ham, cucumber slices, and onion rings in a large bowl, then pour the dressing over them. Gently stir and toss to make sure the dressing is well absorbed into the salad ingredients.

Transfer to a serving bowl and garnish with the cilantro.

PER SERVING: 209 CALORIES, 5.3G FAT, 1.9G SATURATED FAT, 27.6G TOTAL PROTEIN, 76MG CALCIUM, 3,370MG SODIUM

crispy roast duck salad with shredded carrots and cabbage

One summer I added a few new dishes to my restaurant menu that would be suitable for the hot weather. This dish was one of them.

½ lb roasted boneless skinless duck breast, thinly sliced
Flour, for coating
Vegetable oil, for deep-frying
9oz (about ½ a small head) green cabbage cored and thinly sliced
⅔ cup carrots, cut into matchsticks
2 garlic cloves, crushed
2 Thai chilies, lightly crushed
½ tablespoon sugar
¼ cup Thai fish sauce
⅓ cup plus 1 tablespoon freshly squeezed lemon juice
A few cilantro sprigs, for garnishing

Serves 2

Sprinkle the duck slices with a little water, then coat them with the flour, shaking off any excess.

Heat enough oil for deep-frying in a wok over a high heat until it reaches 350°F.

Add the duck slices and deep-fry for about 1–2 minutes, stirring them around, until they become golden brown and crisp. Use a slotted spoon to remove the duck slices from the oil and drain them well on paper towels.

Mix the cabbage and carrots together in a bowl, then add the garlic, chilies, sugar, fish sauce, and lemon juice, and toss together again until well combined.

Transfer the salad to a serving bowl and scatter the crispy duck on top, then garnish with the cilantro sprigs.

PER SERVING: 557 CALORIES, 36G FAT, 5.8G SATURATED FAT, 33.1G TOTAL PROTEIN, 33MG CALCIUM, 2,430MG SODIUM

fragrant ground pork on lemongrass stalks

Pork is quite affordable and can be very tasty if prepared well with the right ingredients. The "skewers" for this recipe are lemongrass stalks, which lend extra flavor and aroma to the finished dish.

14oz (about 1¾ cups) ground pork
2 tablespoons coconut cream
2 teaspoons ready-made Thai red curry paste
1 egg yolk
2 teaspoons shredded kaffir lime leaves
12 lemongrass stalks
½ handful of basil leaves, for garnishing
Lemon and lime zest, for garnishing
Sweet chili and garlic sauce (see page 60, or use ready-made), for serving

Serves 4

Preheat the broiler or heat the barbecue.

Mix together the ground pork, coconut cream, red curry paste, egg yolk, and kaffir lime leaves in a bowl. Using your hands, gently pack an equal amount of the mixture onto each of the lemongrass stalks.

Broil or barbecue the ground pork on lemongrass stalks for 10–15 minutes until cooked, turning occasionally.

Serve garnished with the basil leaves and lemon and lime zest, and accompanied by the sweet chili and garlic sauce.

PER SERVING: 218 CALORIES, 14.6G FAT, 6.3G SATURATED FAT, 20.7G TOTAL PROTEIN, 29MG CALCIUM, 100MG SODIUM

3

soups and
one-plate meals

carrot and sweet potato soup

The color of this soup is incredible—when I see it I feel like diving into the soup bowl! Both the color and texture are so inviting and, of course, the taste is unmistakable for its natural sweetness.

2 teaspoons vegan margarine or
   1 tablespoon extra virgin olive oil
½ onion, chopped
2 large carrots, chopped
1 medium sweet potato, peeled and chopped
2½ cups vegetable broth
3½ tablespoons soy cream
Salt and pepper
1 tablespoon chopped cilantro leaves

Serves 2

Heat the margarine or olive oil in a saucepan over medium heat. Stir in the onion, carrots, and sweet potato, and cook for about 4 minutes.

Add the vegetable broth, bring to a boil, and simmer for 25 minutes until the carrots and sweet potatoes are soft. Remove from the heat and let cool slightly.

Puree the soup in a blender until smooth and creamy. Return it to the pan, stir in the soy cream and reheat. Season with salt and pepper to taste, add the cilantro, and serve hot.

PER SERVING: 198 CALORIES, 9.3G FAT, 1.6G SATURATED FAT, 4.1G TOTAL PROTEIN, 120MG CALCIUM, 590MG SODIUM

green pea soup

This is one soup that I never serve with any bread. I like its richness. It's a good idea to reserve a few whole peas to add to the soup just before serving, to give it extra texture. The crispy bacon provides another dimension: it is fairly salty, so be careful how much salt you add to the soup.

2 teaspoons vegan margarine
½ white onion, chopped
2¼ cups vegetable broth
18oz (about 3½–5 cups) fresh green peas
3½ tablespoons soy milk
Salt and pepper
1 tablespoon chopped parsley
2 tablespoons soy cream (optional)
3 strips of bacon, cut into small pieces and fried until crisp

Serves 2

Melt the margarine in a large saucepan and stir in the onion. Cook until it is light golden, add the broth and bring to a boil. Add the peas, return to a boil, and simmer for a few minutes or until the peas are tender and soft. Remove from the heat.

Add the soy milk, let cool slightly, then puree the soup in a blender until smooth and creamy.

Return the soup to the pan and gently reheat. Season to taste and stir in the parsley. Pour into individual serving bowls, top each with 1 tablespoon of soy cream, twirled in the center (if using), and sprinkle with crispy bacon.

PER SERVING: 342 CALORIES, 12.7G FAT, 4.1G SATURATED FAT, 27.6G TOTAL PROTEIN, 0.8G SOY PROTEIN, 105MG CALCIUM, 1,080MG SODIUM

spicy triple-flavor noodle soup with broccoli and bean sprouts

I call this triple flavor soup because it really does live up to its name. It is healthy and easy to prepare. Once you have tried it, you will be hooked!

5oz (about 2½–3 cups) dried wide rice noodles, soaked
    in cold water for an hour and drained
2¼ cups bean sprouts
3½ cups vegetable broth
2 garlic cloves, lightly pounded
2 fresh cilantro roots, lightly pounded
1½ cups broccoli florets, cut into bite-size pieces
¼ cup Thai fish sauce
2 tablespoons sugar
2 tablespoons distilled malt vinegar
2 tablespoons crushed peanuts
1 fresh red chili, sliced into fine rings
3 tablespoons freshly squeezed lemon juice
½ teaspoon chili powder (optional)
Cilantro leaves, for garnishing

Serves 2

Bring a saucepan of water to a boil over a high heat. Add the noodles and continue boiling for about 1 minute, until the noodles are soft, then immediately add the bean sprouts. Leave for about 15 seconds, then drain well. Transfer the noodles and bean sprouts to 2 individual serving bowls and set aside.

Bring the broth to a boil in the same saucepan and add the pounded garlic, cilantro roots, and broccoli. Reduce the heat and simmer for about 2 minutes, until the garlic and cilantro roots release their aroma. Season the soup with the fish sauce, sugar, vinegar, peanuts, and chili rings.

Divide the soup equally between the bowls, immediately adding the lemon juice and chili powder (if using) to each serving. Garnish with the cilantro leaves and serve.

PER SERVING: 465 CALORIES, 7.9G FAT, 1.4G SATURATED FAT, 17.7G TOTAL PROTEIN, 137MG CALCIUM, 2,880MG SODIUM

pumpkin and basil soup

The Thais use a lot of pumpkin in their cooking which is why I was inspired to create this healthy and tasty soup. Pumpkins from different parts of the world vary hugely in texture (those from Thailand can be quite hard), and cooking times differ accordingly.

4 cups water
14oz (about 3½ cups) pumpkin (peeled and seeded weight),
    cut into chunks
2 potatoes, peeled and chopped
Salt and pepper
¼ cup extra virgin olive oil
1 garlic clove, finely sliced
2 shallots, finely chopped
6 basil leaves, chopped

Serves 2

Bring the water to a boil in a large pan. Add the pumpkin and potato pieces and cook over a low heat until tender.

Mash the pumpkin and potato with a fork to thicken the soup and keep simmering. Season to taste with salt and pepper.

Meanwhile, in another saucepan, heat the oil, add the garlic and shallots, and stir-fry until the garlic is golden. Pour the garlic, shallots, and oil into the soup, add the basil, stir well, and serve.

PER SERVING: 390 CALORIES, 30.2G FAT, 4.2G SATURATED FAT, 4.4G TOTAL PROTEIN, 71MG CALCIUM, 100MG SODIUM

shredded omelet in mild broth

In Thailand this is called poor man's soup. I'll tell you, though, that if a poor man's food tastes this good, I'll swap places with him for a while. It's mild and gentle, yet full of flavor.

2½ cups vegetable broth or water
1 fresh cilantro root, lightly pounded
6oz (about 1¼ cups) cucumber, cut in half, seeded,
   and roughly chopped
⅓ cup onion, coarsely chopped
2 tablespoons Thai fish sauce
1½ teaspoons sugar
2 scallions, cut into 1-inch lengths
2 tablespoons cilantro leaves
Pinch of ground black pepper

For the shredded omelet
1 tablespoon vegetable oil
1 egg, beaten

For the crispy garlic
1 tablespoon vegetable oil
2 garlic cloves, finely crushed

Serves 2

To make the shredded omelet for the garnish, heat the oil in a frying pan over medium-high heat and swirl the oil to cover the whole surface of the pan. Pour in the egg and swirl it around the pan to form a thin layer. Cook until the omelet is set, then tip it out of the pan. Roll up the omelet into a tight cylinder, and cut it across into thin strips. Set aside.

To make the crispy garlic, heat the oil, add the garlic, and fry over a low heat until it is golden and crisp. Drain well on paper towels and set aside.

Place the broth or water in a saucepan over a high heat and bring to a boil. Add the cilantro root, reduce the heat to low, and simmer for 10 minutes. Increase the heat to medium and add the cucumber and onion. Season with the fish sauce and sugar, stir well, and let it simmer for another 3 minutes.

Add the scallions, then transfer the soup to individual serving bowls. Scatter the shredded omelet on top, sprinkle with the crispy garlic, cilantro leaves, and pepper, then serve.

PER SERVING: 88 CALORIES, 7G FAT, 1G SATURATED FAT, 3G TOTAL PROTEIN, 37MG CALCIUM, 320MG SODIUM

clam chowder

Fresh clams are usually available all year round, but canned clams would work in this recipe as well. Soy milk and arrowroot replace the cream in this version of New England clam chowder.

½ tablespoon vegetable oil
½ leek, chopped
½ onion, chopped
2 medium potatoes, peeled and cubed
⅔ cup vegetable broth
6½ oz fresh clams
1 teaspoon arrowroot
Scant cup soy milk
Salt and pepper
2 cilantro sprigs

Serves 2

Heat the oil in a large saucepan, add the leek and onion, and cook for a few minutes until soft. Add the potatoes and cook for another 3 minutes, stirring frequently.

Pour in the broth and let it simmer for about 25 minutes until the vegetables are soft.

Add the clams and arrowroot and simmer and stir for another 5 minutes until the clams are heated through and the chowder has thickened.

Stir in the soy milk and reheat gently. Season with salt and pepper, pour into individual serving bowls, and garnish each one with a cilantro sprig.

PER SERVING: 258 CALORIES, 5.5G FAT, 0.7G SATURATED FAT, 23.7G TOTAL PROTEIN, 3G SOY PROTEIN, 127MG CALCIUM, 1,540MG SODIUM

pasta and chickpea soup

I don't often use chickpeas in my cooking because of the overnight-soaking bit. But you could say to me that sticky rice needs the same soaking time and you are absolutely right. I suppose it's all about forward planning!

¾ cup dried chickpeas, soaked overnight and drained
2 tablespoons chopped fresh rosemary
3 garlic cloves, chopped
3 tablespoons extra virgin olive oil
2½ cups water
1½ cups mostaccioli (quills) pasta
Salt and pepper

Serves 2

Combine the chickpeas, rosemary, garlic, half the olive oil, and the water in a saucepan. Bring to a boil, lower the heat, and simmer for about 1½ hours or until the chickpeas are soft.

Remove from the heat and let cool a little. Transfer the chickpeas to a food processor and whizz to a puree. Return it to the pan and gently reheat.

Meanwhile, bring a large pot of salted water to a boil. Add the pasta and cook until it is al dente, then drain.

Add the cooked pasta to the hot chickpea soup, season to taste, and serve.

PER SERVING: 622 CALORIES, 21.5G FAT, 3.9G SATURATED FAT, 23G TOTAL PROTEIN, 140MG CALCIUM, 130MG SODIUM

plantain and herb soup with chicken

Plantains resemble large bananas. They usually look bruised and battered, but inside, once the skin is peeled off, they have amazing blushed-pink flesh that is delicious when cooked.

3 cups water
2 fresh cilantro roots, lightly pounded
4 kaffir lime leaves, torn
2 lemongrass stalks, lightly pounded
½-inch piece of galangal, finely sliced
   into very thin rounds
4½ tablespoons Thai fish sauce
2 teaspoons sugar
11oz boneless chicken breast, thinly sliced
1 plantain, peeled and cut into ¼-inch-thick slices
4 plum tomatoes, quartered
1 onion, quartered
2 large dried chilies, deep-fried in hot oil for 1 minute,
   drained, and each cut across into 4 pieces
¼ cup freshly squeezed lemon juice
Cilantro leaves, for garnishing

Serves 2

Bring the water to a boil in a saucepan over a high heat. Reduce the heat to low, add the cilantro roots, kaffir lime leaves, lemongrass, and galangal, and simmer for about 10 minutes, until the herbs have released their aroma.

Stir in the fish sauce and sugar, then add the chicken, plantain, tomatoes, and onion. Turn up the heat and continue simmering until the chicken is well cooked. Turn off the heat and add the chilies and lemon juice.

Transfer the soup into individual serving bowls and garnish with the cilantro leaves.

PER SERVING: 394 CALORIES, 4.3G FAT, 0.9G SATURATED FAT, 45.1G TOTAL PROTEIN, 82MG CALCIUM, 2,720MG SODIUM

chicken soup with straw mushrooms and toasted sesame seeds

This is a very simple, light, and soothing soup. If you would like to turn it into a more substantial dish, all you have to do is to add some boiled rice or egg noodles.

3½ cups chicken broth
5½ oz boneless chicken breast, thinly sliced
2 tablespoons light soy sauce
Salt, to taste
1 teaspoon black peppercorns
2 thumb-size pieces of fresh ginger, lightly crushed
6 chestnut mushrooms, washed and trimmed
6 straw mushrooms, drained, squeezed dry,
   and sliced into thin strips
1 scallion, finely sliced into rings
1 teaspoon sesame seeds, toasted over
   a low heat until golden brown
2 tablespoons cilantro leaves

Serves 2

Bring the chicken broth to a boil in a saucepan, and add the soy sauce, salt to taste, peppercorns, and ginger, cover with a lid, and let it simmer for about 5 minutes.

Add the chicken slices and simmer for 2 minutes. Then add both types of mushrooms and simmer for a couple more minutes until the chicken is cooked but still tender.

Transfer the soup into individual serving bowls, discarding the ginger, and sprinkle with the scallion, toasted sesame seeds, and cilantro leaves.

PER SERVING: 146 CALORIES, 2.9G FAT, 0.5G SATURATED FAT, 23.1G TOTAL PROTEIN, 111MG CALCIUM, 1,760MG SODIUM

asparagus soufflé

The asparagus gives this soufflé a really vibrant color. If you've never tried making a soufflé before, then try this recipe—it is a real gem.

12 asparagus spears
Scant cup soy milk
½ onion, thinly sliced
¼ cup scallion, finely chopped
½ red pepper, sliced into strips

1¾ tablespoons vegan
   margarine, plus extra for
   greasing
2 tablespoons flour
Salt and ground white pepper
4 eggs, separated, and
   1 egg white

Serves 2

Cut 4 of the asparagus tips into 3 pieces each, blanch for 1 minute, and set aside. Boil the remaining asparagus in water for a few minutes until tender, drain well, and let cool. Blend the boiled asparagus in a blender until smooth, then rub through a fine strainer to make a puree. Set aside. Put the soy milk in a saucepan with the onion, scallion, red pepper, and blanched asparagus tips. Bring slowly to a boil, remove from the heat, cover, and let infuse for 30 minutes. Strain the soy milk from the vegetables and set both aside.

Preheat the oven to 350°F. Grease a 1½-quart soufflé dish. Melt the margarine in a pan, stir in the flour, and cook gently for a minute, stirring. Remove the saucepan from the heat and stir in the strained soy milk. Bring slowly to a boil and continue to cook, stirring, until the sauce thickens. Stir in the asparagus puree, season to taste, and set aside to cool slightly. Beat the egg yolks into the cooled sauce one at a time.

Using clean beaters, beat the egg whites until they stand in soft peaks. Mix 1 large spoonful of egg white into the sauce to lighten its texture, pour the sauce over the remaining egg whites and gently fold in. Pour the mixture into the prepared dish, smooth the surface with a pastry spatula, and scatter the cooked vegetables on top. Place the soufflé dish on a baking sheet and bake for 30 minutes until the soufflé is golden brown, well risen, and just firm to the touch. Serve hot.

PER SERVING: 431 CALORIES, 27.8G FAT, 6.3G SATURATED FAT, 25.9G TOTAL PROTEIN, 3G SOY PROTEIN, 160MG CALCIUM, 450MG SODIUM

pad thai with coconut milk

Pad Thai is Thailand's most famous and popular fried noodle dish. It is not generally made with coconut milk, but this adds extra flavor, so do try it. If you think that you still prefer the usual recipe, simply omit the coconut milk next time you make it.

1 tablespoon vegetable oil
6 raw black tiger shrimp,
   peeled, deveined and
   de-headed; tails left on
3 tablespoons cooked, miniature
   shrimp
1 egg
3½ oz dried rice vermicelli,
   soaked in cold water for
   1 hour and drained
1½ tablespoons Thai fish sauce
1½ tablespoons distilled
   malt vinegar
¼ cup coconut milk

2 scallions, cut into
   1-inch lengths
1 small carrot, cut into
   matchsticks
1½ cups bean sprouts
1½ tablespoons crushed
   roasted peanuts
1 tablespoon crushed pickled
   turnip (hoa chai-pho), optional
1½ tablespoons sugar
2 lime wedges, for serving
Chili powder (optional)
Cilantro leaves, for garnishing

Serves 2

Heat a wok over a high heat. Add the oil, reduce the heat to medium, add the shrimp and stir-fry for about 30 seconds until they are half-cooked. Add the miniature shrimp, crack in the egg, and keep turning until the egg is well done and looks like uneven, broken pieces of a cooked omelet.

Immediately stir in the noodles, season with the fish sauce and vinegar, and continue stir-frying, constantly tossing and turning the ingredients, but taking care not to break the noodles. Add the coconut milk and stir well, using the corner of a spatula so the noodles don't break.

Add the scallions, most of the carrot, and most of the bean sprouts, some of the peanuts, the turnip, and sugar, stirring until all the ingredients are well blended. Divide the noodles between 2 plates. Garnish with the reserved carrot, bean sprouts, peanuts, and lime wedges. Sprinkle with a little chili powder (if using) and cilantro leaves, and serve.

PER SERVING: 477 CALORIES, 18.8G FAT, 6.6G SATURATED FAT, 21.3G TOTAL PROTEIN, 135MG CALCIUM, 1,510MG SODIUM

baked pineapple rice and roasted pine nuts

This is supposed to be a Thai-style savory rice. However, adding ingredients such as pine nuts and raisins makes it a little more Western—and the baking method really makes this rice cosmopolitan.

1 large pineapple
1 tablespoon pine nuts
2 tablespoons vegetable oil
1 tablespoon frozen peas
2 tablespoons diced carrot
1 tablespoon raisins
2 eggs
14oz (about 3–3½ cups) steamed rice *
Salt, to taste
1½ tablespoons light soy sauce
Ground white pepper
1 chopped red chili, for garnishing

Serves 2

Preheat the oven to 300°F.

Cut the pineapple in half lengthways and scoop out the flesh. Chop half the flesh into small chunks and reserve for use in this recipe; the remaining flesh can be used in another dish—perhaps a refreshing dessert.

Dry-fry the pine nuts in a frying pan until golden brown, then remove from the pan and set aside. Heat the oil in the same pan and stir-fry the pineapple chunks, peas, carrot, raisins, and pine nuts. Add the eggs, breaking the yolks, and continue to stir-fry with the rest of ingredients until well cooked.

Stir in the rice, mix well with the other ingredients, season with salt to taste, and the light soy sauce, and remove from the heat. Divide the rice equally between the pineapple shells, cover with foil, and bake in the oven for 10–15 minutes.

Serve sprinkled with ground white pepper and garnished with the chili slices.

PER SERVING: 606 CALORIES, 24.1G FAT, 3.7G SATURATED FAT, 15.1G TOTAL PROTEIN, 91MG CALCIUM, 1,000MG SODIUM

* If you've no steamed rice already made, then you'll need to prepare some, and 1 cup uncooked rice will yield enough for this recipe (see page 40).

* If you've no boiled rice already made, then you'll have to prepare some, and ½ cup uncooked rice will yield enough for this recipe.

thai savory rice pudding with tiger shrimp and crispy garlic

Most Thai people would have this soup for breakfast when on vacation in the summer at their beach houses by the sea. It's usually made with ground pork, but this shrimp version is equally good.

3½ cups chicken broth
2 fresh cilantro roots,
    lightly pounded
2 cups boiled rice
    (see page 49) *
8oz black tiger shrimp,
    peeled and deveined,
    tails left on

1 teaspoon sugar
2 tablespoons Thai fish sauce
2 eggs
1 thumb-size piece of fresh ginger
    peeled and cut into matchsticks
Crispy garlic (see page 75)
1 scallion, chopped
½ teaspoon ground white pepper
Cilantro leaves, for garnishing

Serves 2

Put the chicken broth in a saucepan, add the pounded cilantro roots and bring to a boil, then discard the cilantro roots and add the cooked rice. Remove from the heat and let it cool slightly.

Transfer to a food processor and blend until the grains have broken up to form a paste. Pour back into the saucepan and bring to a boil. Add the shrimp and season with the sugar and fish sauce. Cook over a high heat for about 2 minutes. (Water can be added if you like the soup quite watery, but in this case, remember to increase the amount of seasoning.)

Pour the soup into individual serving bowls. Crack an egg into each bowl and stir so that the egg cooks in the hot soup. Scatter with the ginger matchsticks and crispy garlic.

Sprinkle with the scallion, ground white pepper, and cilantro leaves.

PER SERVING: 391 CALORIES, 13.5G FAT, 2.5G SATURATED FAT, 34.2G TOTAL PROTEIN, 201MG CALCIUM, 2,000MG SODIUM

seafood and glass noodle casserole

This is a very gingery and aromatic dish. I always find that sesame oil and ginger go very well together. If you can't get hold of fermented soybeans, use 2 tablespoons of light soy sauce.

5½ oz dried glass noodles (cellophane vermicelli), soaked in water for 10 minutes and drained
6 straw mushrooms, squeezed dry and sliced into thin strips
2 fresh cilantro roots, lightly pounded
2 garlic cloves, lightly pounded
½ thumb-size piece of fresh ginger, peeled and cut into matchsticks
1 tablespoon light soy sauce
1 tablespoon fermented soybeans
2 tablespoons sesame oil
1¼ cups chicken broth
6 crab claws
6 medium headless raw shrimp, peeled and deveined
1 scallion, chopped
½ teaspoon ground white pepper
2 tablespoons chopped cilantro, including the stems
Sweet chili and garlic sauce, for serving (optional), see page 60, or use ready-made

Serves 2

Mix the soaked noodles with the mushrooms, cilantro roots, garlic, ginger, soy sauce, soybeans (if using), and sesame oil. Set aside.

Put the chicken broth in a casserole dish or other heatproof container—one which will fit into the top compartment of a steamer, followed by the crab claws, shrimp, and seasoned glass noodles. Cover with a lid and cook in a preheated steamer for about 10 minutes.

Use a pair of tongs to mix all the ingredients well, bringing the shrimp and crab claws to the top. Sprinkle with the scallion and pepper, and steam for another 2–3 minutes. Sprinkle with the chopped cilantro leaves and serve, if you wish, with sweet chili and garlic sauce.

PER SERVING: 501 CALORIES, 15.7G FAT, 2.1G SATURATED FAT, 27.4G TOTAL PROTEIN, 2G SOY PROTEIN, 84MG CALCIUM, 1,650MG SODIUM

rice with smoked halibut and thyme

The first time I made this I was trying to impress someone—and, boy, did it work! Smoked halibut is not cheap, but you only need a small quantity, so why not treat yourself.

1 tablespoon olive oil
6oz (a scant cup) rice, soaked in water for 30 minutes, and well drained
3½ oz (about ½–⅔ cup) smoked halibut, cut into small pieces
1 cup green cabbage, roughly sliced and the layers separated
1 thyme sprig, leaves only
2 cups water
Salt and pepper

Serves 2

Put the olive oil, rice, and smoked halibut in a heavy pan and stir to mix well. Top with the cabbage, add the thyme, and gently pour the water over the cabbage.

Cover the pan, bring to a boil, and simmer for 15–20 minutes until all the liquid has been absorbed. Then stir gently and season with salt and pepper. Raise the heat to high for about 15 seconds, still with the lid on the pan.

Remove from the heat, keeping the lid on, and let the rice stand for another 5–7 minutes before serving.

PER SERVING: 398 CALORIES, 6.7G FAT, 0.8G SATURATED FAT, 15.4G TOTAL PROTEIN, 38MG CALCIUM, 480MG SODIUM

baked marinated sea bass with mashed sweet potatoes

Mashed sweet potatoes are a delicious alternative to the traditional mash, and you can achieve the same texture without having to use milk or butter. It goes extremely well with the rosemary-scented sea bass.

4 garlic cloves, lightly crushed
10 mixed olives
Zest of 1 lemon
2 tablespoons extra virgin olive oil
Salt and black pepper
2 sea bass fillets
2 rosemary stems

For the mashed sweet potatoes
3 medium sweet potatoes, peeled and chopped
2 tablespoons extra virgin olive oil
Chopped parsley, for garnishing

Serves 2

Preheat the oven to 400°F.

In a large bowl, gently mix together the garlic, olives, lemon zest, olive oil, and salt and pepper. Place the fish in an ovenproof dish and pour the mixture over it. Top with the rosemary and bake in the oven for 20 minutes.

Meanwhile, bring a large pot of water to a boil and add the sweet potato pieces. Reduce the heat and simmer until the potatoes are tender. Gently drain off the water and transfer the potato to a mixing bowl. Add the olive oil and mash well, seasoning with salt and pepper, to taste.

Serve with the sea bass and the olive and rosemary sauce. Garnish with the parsley.

PER SERVING: 479 CALORIES, 26.8G FAT, 4G SATURATED FAT, 22.4G TOTAL PROTEIN, 195MG CALCIUM, 570MG SODIUM

broiled salmon steaks with creamy lemon sauce

You will be surprised how delicious the sauce in this dish tastes, despite the usual cream being replaced by soy cream. Serve with steamed green vegetables or a fresh crispy salad.

½ tablespoon olive oil
1 garlic clove, pounded with ½ fresh cilantro root to make a paste
Salt and pepper
2 salmon fillets, weighing about 9oz each

For the sauce
½ tablespoon vegan margarine
2 garlic cloves, crushed
½ cup chicken broth
⅓ cup plus 1 tablespoon soy cream
¼ cup freshly squeezed lemon juice
2 tablespoons finely chopped basil leaves

Serves 2

First make the sauce. Heat the margarine, add the garlic, and stir-fry for a few minutes over medium heat. Add the chicken broth, soy cream, and lemon juice, then bring to a boil. Reduce the heat to low and simmer gently.

Meanwhile, preheat the broiler to high and oil the broiler rack. Season the garlic and cilantro paste with salt and pepper, to taste, and spread it on both sides of the salmon. Broil the fish for about 3 minutes on each side or until it is cooked to your liking.

Transfer the salmon to individual serving plates. Add the basil to the sauce, season with salt and pepper, and pour the sauce over the salmon.

PER SERVING: 381 CALORIES, 28.5G FAT, 5.1G SATURATED FAT, 28G TOTAL PROTEIN, 100MG CALCIUM, 310MG SODIUM

monkfish skewers with coconut milk curry sauce

The texture of monkfish is like that of steak; it does not flake like other types of fish. This makes it extremely versatile—you can cook it in all kinds of ways and it keeps its shape. It is great for kebabs like these.

2 tablespoons vegetable oil
1 tablespoon ready-made
　Thai red curry paste
2 tablespoons freshly squeezed
　lemon juice
2 teaspoons Thai fish sauce
1 teaspoon sugar
1 tablespoon chopped basil
1lb monkfish fillet,
　cut into 12 cubes

Boiled rice (see page 49),
　for serving

For the sauce
1 tablespoon ready-made
　Thai red curry paste
⅓ cup plus 1 tablespoon
　coconut milk
½ teaspoon sugar
6 basil leaves

Serves 2

Mix 1 tablespoon of the oil with the curry paste, lemon juice, fish sauce, sugar, and basil in a large bowl. Add the cubes of fish, stirring so they are well coated, cover with plastic wrap and place in the fridge to marinate for 15 minutes.

Preheat the broiler to high and use the remaining oil to grease the broiler rack. Thread 6 cubes of monkfish onto each of 2 bamboo skewers, about 9 inches long, which have been soaked in water. Place the skewers on the rack under the broiler for about 3 minutes, turning them occasionally, until the fish has cooked through.

Meanwhile, put all the sauce ingredients except the basil leaves in a small saucepan and cook over medium heat, stirring frequently, until well mixed, smooth, and heated through. Add the basil leaves, and stir for another 15 seconds.

Serve the monkfish skewers with boiled rice and drizzle the rice with the coconut milk curry sauce.

PER SERVING: 333 CALORIES, 17.2G FAT, 7.9G SATURATED FAT, 37.2G TOTAL PROTEIN, 70MG CALCIUM, 470MG SODIUM

dried chicken curry with warm pita bread

One day I ran out of rice at home but I had some red curry with chicken left from the night before. I went to the store and bought some pita bread to eat with the curry. It turned out to be one of the best lunches I've had in years!

1 tablespoon vegetable oil
1½ tablespoons ready-made Thai red curry paste
3 kaffir lime leaves, torn
⅓ cup plus 1 tablespoon coconut cream
⅓ cup plus 1 tablespoon soy milk
7oz boneless skinless chicken, thinly sliced along the grain
1½ teaspoons Thai fish sauce
1½ teaspoons sugar
Handful of snow peas
2 large pita breads, warmed
4 sweet basil leaves, chopped
1 red chili, thinly sliced lengthways

Serves 2

Heat the oil in a wok over a low heat. Add the curry paste and lime leaves and stir-fry for about 15 seconds, taking care not to burn the mixture.

Slowly stir in the coconut cream and soy milk, then add the chicken, increase the heat to medium, and cook until the chicken is cooked. If the sauce seems to be drying out, add a small amount of water to keep everything moist, but do not make the sauce too thin. Season with the fish sauce and sugar. Add the snow peas and stir around for a minute or so.

Pile the dried chicken curry into the warmed pita breads and sprinkle with the basil leaves and chili slices before serving.

PER SERVING: 448 CALORIES, 14.8G FAT, 10.3G SATURATED FAT, 34.9G TOTAL PROTEIN, 1.5G SOY PROTEIN, 213MG CALCIUM, 560MG SODIUM

pan-fried chicken breast with creamy basil sauce

Skinless chicken breasts are relatively low in fat and therefore go well with a richer kind of sauce. This sauce is creamy without using dairy cream, and is, in fact, quite light. Serve with vegetables of your choice.

1 tablespoon flour
Salt and pepper
2 large skinless boneless chicken breasts
2 teaspoons olive oil
2 teaspoons vegan margarine
2 basil sprigs, for garnishing

For the basil cream sauce
2 teaspoons vegan margarine
1 garlic clove, crushed
¼ cup chicken broth or water
¼ cup soy cream
2 tablespoons freshly squeezed lemon juice
1 tablespoon finely chopped basil leaves

Serves 2

Put the flour in a bowl and season with a little salt and pepper. Coat the chicken breasts in the flour, shaking off any excess.

Heat the oil and margarine in a frying pan, add the chicken, and cook over medium heat for 5 minutes on each side or until golden and cooked through. Remove from the pan and keep warm.

Meanwhile, make the sauce. Heat the margarine in the same pan, add the garlic, and cook for a couple of minutes. Add the chicken broth or water, soy cream, and lemon juice, then bring to a boil. Lower the heat, add the chopped basil leaves, and season with salt and pepper, to taste.

Place each chicken breast on a serving plate and pour the sauce over it. Garnish each with a sprig of basil and serve.

PER SERVING: 349 CALORIES, 18.7G FAT, 3.5G SATURATED FAT, 38.2G TOTAL PROTEIN, 63MG CALCIUM, 320MG SODIUM

steamed chicken and ginger rice

This has been a favorite dish of mine since I was eight years old. I just love the aroma that fills the kitchen as you cook the rice. You must eat it with chilled cucumber slices, otherwise it's like having toast without butter and jam.

1 teaspoon vegetable oil
1 teaspoon crushed garlic
2⅓ cups rice, washed and well drained
½ chicken, about 18oz, half the skin trimmed off
5 cups water
½ teaspoon salt
2 fresh cilantro roots, pounded
A thumb-size piece of fresh ginger, cut in
   half and lightly pounded (do not peel)
Chilled cucumber slices
Cilantro leaves, for garnishing

For the sauce
1 teaspoon fresh ginger paste
1 teaspoon finely chopped garlic
½ teaspoon sugar
3 Thai chilies, finely chopped
2 tablespoons fermented soybeans
1 tablespoon chicken broth

To season the soup
½ tablespoon light soy sauce, or to taste
Pinch of ground white pepper
2 scallions, finely chopped

Serves 2

In a frying pan, heat the oil and fry the garlic until it releases its aroma. Add the rice grains and fry with the garlic and oil until mixed well, then set aside.

Put the chicken in a saucepan with the water and bring to a boil. Simmer for about 30 minutes until you have a well-flavored broth and the chicken is cooked. Reserve a tablespoon for the sauce.

Steam the garlic rice in an electric rice cooker using 3⅔ cups of the chicken broth and adding the pounded cilantro roots and ginger. If you don't have a rice cooker, place the rice, broth, cilantro roots, and ginger in a heavy pan, cover with a tight-fitting lid, and bring to a boil. Reduce the heat to low and simmer for 15–20 minutes until all the broth is absorbed. Remove the pan from the heat and let it stand for 5–7 minutes, still with the lid on.

To make the sauce, mix all the ingredients for the sauce together, stir well, and set aside.

Remove the chicken from the rest of the broth. Strip the chicken off the bones and chop the meat into small pieces. Discard the bones. Keep the chicken broth to make a mild soup to accompany the rice (see below).

Scoop the cooked rice onto a serving plate, discarding the ginger lumps and cilantro roots, then arrange the chicken on top, along with the cucumber slices and a sprinkling of cilantro leaves. Serve the sauce in a separate dish.

Reheat the chicken broth, season with the light soy sauce and ground white pepper, sprinkle with the chopped scallions, and serve with the rice.

PER SERVING: 494 CALORIES, 7G FAT, 1.4G SATURATED FAT, 38.8G TOTAL PROTEIN, 4G SOY PROTEIN, 37MG CALCIUM, 1,530MG SODIUM

broiled curried sausages with herbal accompaniments

Ready-made sausages often contain dairy products, so here is an easy recipe for making your own— Thai-style. Serve with the mash and "gravy" on the right for my interpretation of the classic British dish, bangers and mash.

18oz ground pork
2 tablespoons lemongrass, finely chopped
1 tablespoon galangal, pounded to a paste
4 kaffir lime leaves, finely chopped
2 red chilies and 2 garlic cloves, blended together
   in a blender or mortar and pestle
2–3 tablespoons ready-made Thai red curry paste
2¼ teaspoons sugar
1½ teaspoons salt
1 teaspoon ground turmeric
Cilantro sprigs, for garnishing
6–8 Thai chilies, sliced
2½-inch piece of fresh ginger, peeled
   and cut into thin matchsticks

Serves 4

Preheat the broiler to high.

Mix the pork well with the next 8 ingredients. Using your hands, form small quantities of the mixture into sausage shapes.

Place the sausages under the broiler for about 10–15 minutes or until the pork is well cooked, turning occasionally.

Serve the sausages garnished with a few cilantro sprigs, the Thai chilies, and ginger. Accompany with the pan-fried mashed potatoes, drizzled with the creamy green curry sauce (see right).

PER SERVING (WITHOUT MASHED POTATOES AND SAUCE): 269 CALORIES, 15.8G FAT, 4.5G SATURATED FAT, 25.4G TOTAL PROTEIN, 43MG CALCIUM, 1070MG SODIUM

pan-fried mashed potatoes with green curry sauce

This is my accompaniment to the broiled curried sausages on the left.

Salt and pepper
2 large potatoes, peeled and cut into small chunks
1 teaspoon chopped fresh ginger and 1 teaspoon
   chopped fresh cilantro root, pounded together
   to make a fine paste
1 tablespoon vegan margarine
½ tablespoon vegetable oil
2 teaspoons ready-made Thai green curry paste
⅔ cup soy cream

Bring a pan of salted water to a boil and add the potatoes. Cook until tender, then drain. Mash the potatoes with half of the ginger and cilantro root paste and season with salt and pepper, to taste.

Brush a non-stick flat-bottomed frying pan with a little margarine and heat. Put a large scoop of mashed potatoes in the middle of the pan and use a spatula to flatten it. Pan-fry until slightly browned and crisp, then carefully turn it over to cook the other side in the same way. Repeat the process with the remaining mashed potatoes.

To make the sauce, heat the oil in a frying pan over medium heat. Stir in the rest of the ginger and cilantro root paste, taking care not to burn it. Add the green curry paste and stir for 10–15 seconds before pouring in the soy cream. Gently stir to blend all the ingredients and let it simmer for 2–3 minutes until the sauce has thickened slightly.

PER SERVING (MASHED POTATOES AND SAUCE ONLY): 208 CALORIES, 11.9G FAT, 1.8G SATURATED FAT, 3.9G TOTAL PROTEIN, 46MG CALCIUM, 190MG SODIUM

broiled marinated lamb chops with fragrant spices

I'm not that familiar with lamb because I was not brought up eating it on a regular basis. However, I enjoy this dish which partners the meat with other aromatic ingredients and a fresh vegetable sauce.

1 teaspoon cumin seeds, lightly toasted and finely ground
1-inch piece of fresh ginger peeled and finely chopped
2 shallots, chopped
2 garlic cloves, chopped
1 lemongrass stalk, chopped
1 tablespoon sugar
½ teaspoon salt
1 tablespoon vegetable oil, plus a little extra for blending

2 double lamb loin chops, trimmed of excess fat

For the sauce
1¾ tablespoons vegan margarine
3 cups leeks, thinly sliced
⅓ cup soy cream
¾ cup frozen peas
Salt and pepper

Serves 2

Put the cumin powder, ginger, shallots, garlic, lemongrass, sugar, and salt in a food processor and whizz to a smooth paste, adding a dash of oil to help the mixture turn. Heat the oil in a pan and stir-fry the paste over a low heat to release the fragrance, then remove from the pan and let cool.

Rub the paste all over the lamb chops and leave, covered, in the fridge to marinate for 30 minutes.

Meanwhile, make the sauce. Heat the margarine in a frying pan and fry the leeks for 10 minutes over medium heat until they are soft. Add the soy cream and bring to a boil. Lower the heat and add the peas, season with salt and pepper, and continue to cook for another 4 minutes.

Preheat the broiler to high. Broil the chops for about 3–4 minutes on each side, or less if you like your lamb quite rare. Serve with the leek and pea sauce.

PER SERVING: 531 CALORIES, 35G FAT, 9.2G SATURATED FAT, 36G TOTAL PROTEIN, 131MG CALCIUM, 710MG SODIUM

ground beef curry with baked potato

Have you ever heard of ragù sauce on baked potatoes? Well, now you have! This is my way of making it, but the meat sauce is more fiery and, I think, tastier than the usual version.

2 large baking potatoes, scrubbed
1 tablespoon vegetable oil
1 cup lean ground beef
1½ tablespoons ready-made Thai red curry paste
⅓ cup coconut milk
⅓ cup soy cream
1½ teaspoons Thai fish sauce
1½ teaspoons sugar
6 basil leaves

Serves 2

Preheat the oven to 350°F.

Wrap the potatoes in foil and bake on the middle shelf of the oven for about 2 hours or until cooked through.

Heat the oil in a wok over medium heat. Add the ground beef and fry, stirring often, until the beef is half cooked. Add the curry paste, followed by the coconut milk and soy cream and stir to mix well. Season with the fish sauce and sugar. Reduce the heat to low and simmer for a couple of minutes. Add the basil leaves and give it one more good stir.

Unwrap the potatoes, split them open, and serve with the curry sauce poured over them.

PER SERVING: 554 CALORIES, 31G FAT, 11G SATURATED FAT, 29G TOTAL PROTEIN, 95MG CALCIUM, 780MG SODIUM

rosemary cheeseburger with plantain chips and tomato salsa

You don't have to go without a cheeseburger just because you're following a dairy-free diet. This one is much tastier than the hamburger-joint version—and far healthier.

1 slice of white bread, crust removed
¾ cup lean ground beef
1 egg yolk, beaten
2 slices of soy cheese
2 sesame bread rolls
Handful of spinach leaves

For the plantain chips
1 plantain
¾ cup flour
1 tablespoon vegetable oil

For the tomato salsa
1 tablespoon olive oil
2 rosemary sprigs, leaves only
2 garlic cloves, finely chopped
2 plum tomatoes, chopped into small pieces
Juice of ½ lemon
Salt and pepper

Serves 2

Make the salsa first of all. In a frying pan, heat the olive oil and fry the rosemary leaves along with the garlic until they release their fragrance. Stir in the tomatoes, cook for another minute, and season with the lemon juice and salt and pepper, to taste. Set aside.

Tear the slice of white bread into small pieces, place in a food processor, and blend into crumbs. In a large bowl, use your hands to mix the beef, egg yolk, and breadcrumbs together, then season with pepper.

Preheat the broiler to high. Shape the mixture into 2 even-sized burgers not more than ⅜-inch thick. Cook the burgers under the broiler for 3 minutes on each side or until cooked to

your liking. Put a slice of cheese on top of each burger and continue to broil until the cheese has melted, then keep warm. Split open the bread rolls and place them, cut side down, on the grill pan or under the broiler to toast them lightly.

Meanwhile, peel the plantain and thinly slice across at an angle. Coat the pieces with the flour. Heat a frying pan, brush with the oil, and fry the plantain pieces in batches for a minute each side, turning once, until golden brown. Set aside.

Arrange some spinach leaves on the bottom half of each bread roll and top with a burger and some tomato salsa. Cover with the top half of each roll and serve alongside the plantain chips.

PER SERVING: 868 CALORIES, 34.7G FAT, 8.1G SATURATED FAT, 40.9G TOTAL PROTEIN, 4.5G SOY PROTEIN, 376MG CALCIUM, 720MG SODIUM

4

main courses

polenta with wild mushrooms and spaghetti squash

This wonderful combination of flavors and textures makes a vegetarian main course that is free from dairy products. Spaghetti squash is an interesting-looking vegetable that should be used more often.

7½ cups water
Salt and ground black pepper
1⅓ cups coarse polenta (cornmeal)
3½ tablespoons vegan margarine
½ spaghetti squash (about 18oz), seeded

Serves 4

For the mushrooms
¼ cup olive oil
1 garlic clove, chopped
18oz wild or cultivated wide-capped mushrooms, quartered
1 tablespoon chopped oregano, plus a few sprigs
⅔ cup dry white wine

Bring the water to a boil in a large pot with 1 teaspoon salt. Gradually add the polenta, letting it run through your fingers in a stream, and stirring constantly to prevent lumps forming. Simmer for 30–35 minutes, continuing to stir, until the mixture comes away from the sides of the pot. Stir in the margarine and add pepper to taste. While the polenta is still hot, spread it on a dampened baking sheet or wooden board to a thickness of about ⅜ inch. Leave for an hour or so or until softly set.

Meanwhile, cook the spaghetti squash in boiling water until just tender. Using a fork, rake out the spaghetti-like strands of flesh and keep warm.

To cook the mushrooms, heat the olive oil in a pan and add the garlic, mushrooms, and chopped oregano. Cook for a few minutes, then add the wine, raise the heat, and continue to cook until the wine has almost completely evaporated. Season to taste and keep warm.

Preheat a grill plan, cut the polenta into triangles and grill on both sides until lightly charred. Serve the polenta immediately, with strings of spaghetti squash and the mushrooms.

PER SERVING: 434 CALORIES, 23.9G FAT, 4G SATURATED FAT, 7.9G TOTAL PROTEIN, 52MG CALCIUM, 640MG SODIUM

stuffed peppers with aromatic rice

A new twist on a classic theme: the filling for these poppers is deliciously flavored with garlic, chili, basil, and soy sauce.

4 red, green, orange, or yellow peppers
¼ cup vegetable oil
4 garlic cloves, pounded with 2 fresh chilies to make a coarse paste
¾ cup cooked rice (see page 49)
1 cup onion, diced
2½ cups spring greens, thinly sliced

3oz (about 1½ cups) broccoli, stalks thinly sliced, florets cut into bite-size pieces
A small handful of snow peas, topped and tailed
4 teaspoons light soy sauce
1 teaspoon dark soy sauce
2 teaspoons white sugar
Salt, to taste
½ handful of holy basil leaves
1 fresh red chili, chopped

Serves 4

Preheat the oven to 375°F.

Cut the tops off the peppers and reserve them to use as "lids". Scoop out the core and seeds and set aside.

Heat a wok or frying pan over medium heat, then add the oil. Add the garlic and chili paste, and stir for a couple of seconds until it releases its aroma. (By heating the wok first, you ensure that the oil won't be so hot that it burns the paste when you add it.) Immediately stir in the cooked rice, followed by the onion, spring greens, broccoli, and snow peas. Season with the soy sauces, sugar, and salt, stirring to distribute the brown color from the soy sauces evenly. Add the holy basil leaves and chopped chili and stir for a few seconds.

Stuff the rice mixture tightly into the peppers. Brush the bottom of a shallow baking dish or roasting pan with a little oil and stand the stuffed peppers in it. Replace the pepper "lids" and bake in the oven for about 20 minutes, until the peppers are soft but still whole. Serve hot.

PER SERVING: 437 CALORIES, 24.5G FAT, 2.6G SATURATED FAT, 10.3G TOTAL PROTEIN, 194MG CALCIUM, 1,110MG SODIUM

baked leeks with fennel and potatoes

I tend to use leeks as I do scallions, but because leeks are thicker and firmer, they are more suitable for baking. I cannot think of any Thai dish that uses leeks; I will have to create one when I have a moment.

14oz fennel bulbs
14oz new potatoes
8oz (about 3¼–3½ cups) leeks, sliced into 3-inch lengths
⅓ cup plus 1 tablespoon olive oil
3 tablespoons vegan margarine, melted
5 teaspoons water
1 lemon
4 thyme sprigs
2 large red onions, cut into rings ¼-inch thick
Salt and pepper

Serves 4

Preheat the oven to 400°F.

Quarter the fennel bulbs and cut the new potatoes in half. Place, cut side up, with the leeks in a large roasting pan, then drizzle with the olive oil, melted margarine, and the small amount of water.

Cut the lemon in half and squeeze the juice from both halves onto the vegetables, then add the squeezed lemon halves to the roasting pan as well. Add the thyme and cover with a dampened sheet of parchment paper or foil.

Cook in the oven for about 20–25 minutes or until the vegetables are tender. About 10 minutes before they are ready, add the red onions to the roasting pan and continue to bake until everything is tender. Season with salt and pepper before serving.

PER SERVING: 387 CALORIES, 29.7G FAT, 4.5G SATURATED FAT, 4.9G TOTAL PROTEIN, 80MG CALCIUM, 180MG SODIUM

carrot and pumpkin risotto

This is a colorful dish and tastes sweet because of the natural sweetness of the carrots and pumpkin. The texture of the pumpkin combined with the rice makes this risotto substantial.

8½ cups vegetable broth
1¾ tablespoons vegan margarine
3 tablespoons olive oil
2 garlic cloves
1 red onion, finely chopped
1⅔ cups carrots, chopped
18oz (about 3½–3¾ cups) pumpkin, peeled,
    seeded and chopped
2⅓ cups risotto rice
Salt and ground black pepper
½ handful of basil leaves, finely chopped

Serves 4

Bring the broth to a boil in a pan, then reduce the heat and keep at a low simmer.

Heat the margarine and olive oil in a large, heavy saucepan over medium heat. Add the garlic and onion, and stir-fry for a couple of minutes, taking care not to burn the garlic. Add the carrots and pumpkin, and cook until soft. Add the rice and stir for a minute with the rest of ingredients until well coated.

Add a ladleful of hot broth and simmer, stirring, until it has been absorbed. Continue to repeat this process, adding a ladleful of hot broth at a time, until the rice is tender but retaining a bite. Season to taste with salt and pepper and stir in the basil leaves.

Remove from the heat, cover, and let stand for about 3–4 minutes. Spoon into warm bowls and serve immediately.

PER SERVING: 552 CALORIES, 14.9G FAT, 2.4G SATURATED FAT, 12.7G TOTAL PROTEIN, 132MG CALCIUM, 810MG SODIUM

massaman curry with quorn and vegetables

One of the few Thai curries that are garnished with cilantro instead of sweet basil, which shows that its roots are in Muslim countries that are neighbors of Thailand. If you can't find Massaman curry paste, use Thai red curry paste.

1 tablespoon vegetable oil
¼ cup Massaman curry paste or Thai red curry paste
11oz Quorn (mycoprotein) chunks (if unavailble, use firm tofu)
Scant cup coconut milk
1¼ cups soy cream
2 large potatoes, peeled and each cut into 4–5 chunks
1 onion, coarsely sliced
1 tablespoon roasted peanuts
4 cardamom seeds, roasted (if using red curry paste)
2 x 1-inch cinnamon sticks, roasted (if using red curry paste)
2 tablespoons tamarind juice or 1½ tablespoons
    freshly squeezed lemon juice
3 tablespoons palm sugar or 1¼ tablespoons sugar
1½ tablespoons Thai fish sauce, or salt to taste (for vegetarians)
½ handful of cilantro leaves, for garnishing
Nan bread or cooked rice (see page 49), for serving

For the crispy shallots
4 shallots, thinly sliced
1 tablespoon vegetable oil

Serves 4

First make the crispy shallots, Heat the oil in a wok over medium heat. Add the shallot slices and fry, stirring, until they turn golden brown and crisp. Remove from the pan and drain well on paper towels. Set aside.

To make the curry, heat the oil in a wok over a low heat. Add the curry paste and stir-fry for about 15 seconds, taking care not to let it burn. Add the Quorn (or tofu) chunks and stir-fry, constantly tossing and turning, for 1 minute.

Stir in the coconut milk and soy cream and simmer, stirring, for 5 minutes, then add the potatoes, onion, peanuts, cardamom seeds, and cinnamon sticks (if using). Season with the tamarind or lemon juice, sugar, and fish sauce or salt. Let the curry simmer for about 20 minutes, or until the potatoes are cooked through and oil starts appearing on the surface of the sauce.

Transfer the curry to a serving bowl and garnish with the crispy shallots and cilantro leaves. Serve alongside nan bread or rice.

PER SERVING: 536 CALORIES, 34.9G FAT, 10.4G SATURATED FAT, 19.7G TOTAL PROTEIN, 153MG CALCIUM, 1,010MG SODIUM

jungle curry with lychees and zucchini

Jungle curry, so called because it was traditionally made with any vegetables that country dwellers had at hand, is actually my most favorite curry of all. It is great for the waistline as well as being very healthy.

¼ cup ready-made Thai red curry paste
1 teaspoon grated kaffir lime zest
1½ tablespoons vegetable oil
5 kaffir lime leaves, torn
3 cups vegetable broth or water
14oz can lychees, drained and
   1 cup of the syrup reserved
11oz (about 1½–1¾ cups) butternut squash,
   peeled and cut into chunks
2 large zucchini
2¾-inch piece of galangal, cut into thin matchsticks
1 tablespoon fresh green peppercorns (see page 120)
¼ cup Thai fish sauce
1 teaspoon sugar
½ handful of holy basil leaves
1 fresh green chili, thinly sliced lengthways
1 fresh red chili, thinly sliced lengthways
Boiled rice (see page 49), for serving

Serves 4

Begin by enhancing the ready-made curry paste. Use a mortar and pestle to pound the grated lime zest and curry paste together. Heat the oil in a wok over a low heat, then add the paste and stir-fry for about 15 seconds until the paste releases its aroma, taking care not to burn it. Add the lime leaves and stir for another 10 seconds.

Add the vegetable broth or water to the wok along with the reserved lychee syrup and bring to a boil, constantly stirring to make sure the curry paste is well mixed with the liquid and there are no lumps.

Lower the heat to medium, add the butternut squash, and cook for 3–4 minutes or until it is tender. Add the zucchini, lychees, galangal, and green peppercorns. Season with the fish sauce and sugar and let it cook for another 2 minutes.

Just before serving, add most of the holy basil leaves and most of the sliced chilies and give the curry one last stir. Transfer to a serving bowl and garnish with the remaining basil and chilies. Serve with boiled rice.

PER SERVING: 217 CALORIES, 8G FAT, 0.6G SATURATED FAT, 6.8G TOTAL PROTEIN, 134MG CALCIUM, 1,620G SODIUM

eggplant with garlic and chili

This dish goes well with most types of pasta or can be served on toasted bruschetta. It also works as a pizza topping, but is better without the usual cheese, so it's ideal for people who are reducing or eliminating dairy products from their diet.

1 large eggplant
1 tablespoon vegetable oil
8 cherry tomatoes, cut in half
2 garlic cloves, pounded with
    1 fresh red chili to make a paste
½ teaspoon sugar
Salt, to taste
¼ cup vegetable broth or water
1 fresh red chili, sliced lengthways
½ handful of basil leaves

Serves 4

Slice the eggplant lengthways into long flat pieces and dip the slices in cold water, then drain on paper towels. Cook in a frying pan over low heat without any oil, turning once, until cooked but still firm. Drain off any excess water, and keep the eggplant slices warm.

Heat the oil in the same pan, add the tomatoes and the garlic and chili paste, and stir-fry for a few seconds, taking care not to let the paste burn. Reduce the heat, season with the sugar, and salt to taste, and pour in the broth or water. Simmer for about 30 seconds or until the sauce has thickened slightly.

Stir in most of the sliced chili and most of the basil leaves, and heat for a few seconds.

Drizzle the sauce over the cooked zucchini and serve garnished with the remaining chili slices and basil leaves.

PER SERVING: 54 CALORIES, 3.4G FAT, 0.3G SATURATED FAT, 1.6G TOTAL PROTEIN, 20MG CALCIUM, 120MG SODIUM

stir-fried assorted mushrooms and baby corn with scallions

I like all kinds of mushrooms and it really surprises me that there are quite a few people who are allergic to them. What a pity! This dish can be served with boiled egg noodles or steamed rice.

2 tablespoons vegetable oil
4 garlic cloves, crushed
4¼ oz oyster
    mushrooms, trimmed
2 cups canned straw
    mushrooms, squeezed dry
    and sliced into thin strips
3oz (1¼–1½ cups) button
    mushrooms, quartered
⅔ cup dried jelly mushrooms
    (ear mushrooms), soaked in
    warm water until soft and
    squeezed dry
8–9 baby corn
¼ cup water
1 tablespoon Thai fish sauce
1 tablespoon light soy sauce
½ teaspoon sugar
2 scallions, cut into 1-inch lengths
1 tablespoon tapioca flour, mixed
    to a paste with 2–3 tablespoons
    cold water
1 tablespoon sesame oil
Pinch of ground white pepper
Cilantro leaves, for garnishing

Serves 4

Heat the oil in a wok over medium heat. Add the crushed garlic and stir around for a few seconds until it releases its fragrance. Add all the mushrooms, along with the baby corn, and stir for a minute or two, then add the water and bring to a boil, stirring constantly.

Reduce the heat and season with the fish sauce, soy sauce, and sugar. Stir in the scallions. Add the tapioca flour paste and stir until the sauce thickens to the consistency of gravy.

Serve sprinkled with ground white pepper and cilantro leaves.

PER SERVING: 177 CALORIES, 8.9G FAT, 1.1G SATURATED FAT, 4.7G TOTAL PROTEIN, 51MG CALCIUM, 600MG SODIUM

poached eggs topped with onion and tomatoes

When I was a little girl, my grandmother told me, with a straight face, that this dish was called "poor man's eggs". I realise now this is because the ingredients are quite cheap, but it is no less enjoyable for that.

Vegetable oil, for frying
1 onion, thinly sliced into rings
3 large plum tomatoes, chopped
3 large new potatoes, chopped
1 large carrot, chopped
2 tablespoons water
1½ tablespoons Thai fish sauce
1 teaspoon distilled malt vinegar
1 teaspoon sugar
8 small eggs
Pinch of ground white pepper

Serves 4

Heat a little oil in a frying pan, add the onion rings, and fry, stirring occasionally, until lightly browned. Stir in the rest of the vegetables, cook for a couple of minutes, and add the water. Cover and simmer until the carrots and potatoes are cooked but still slightly firm—be careful not to overcook them. Season with the fish sauce, vinegar, and sugar, and keep warm.

To poach the eggs, bring a pan of water to a boil. Gently break in the eggs one by one (you will probably have to prepare them in 3 batches). Cook them until the egg whites form (about 4 minutes) or to suit your taste. When the eggs are cooked, use a slotted spoon to lift them gently out of the pan and onto a plate. Keep warm while you cook the remaining eggs in the same way.

Carefully place the poached eggs on a serving plate. Pour the vegetable sauce over them and sprinkle with pepper for serving.

PER SERVING: 347 CALORIES, 21.8G FAT, 4.7G SATURATED FAT, 19.3G TOTAL PROTEIN, 111MG CALCIUM, 650MG SODIUM

seasonal vegetables with couscous

Here I have used couscous instead of the (for me) more usual rice. They do taste very similar but I find couscous has a much finer texture and is not as filling as rice, so it's a good partner for mixed vegetables.

2 cups couscous
2½ cups boiling water
4oz (about 1 cup) baby carrots, chopped
1 red pepper, seeded and thinly sliced
4oz (a large handful) sugar snap peas
4 baby leeks, sliced
4oz (about ¾ cup) corn kernels
¼ cup lemon juice
2 tablespoons olive oil
Salt and pepper
1 tablespoon chopped mint

Serves 4

Put the couscous in a large bowl and cover with the boiling water. Let it stand for 10 minutes or until all the water has been absorbed, then fluff up the couscous grains with a fork.

Cook the carrots in lightly salted boiling water for 2 minutes, then add the red pepper, sugar snap peas, leeks, and corn kernels, and continue to cook for another 3 minutes. Drain well before adding to the couscous.

Add the lemon juice and oil to the bowl and stir in carefully. Season with salt and pepper to taste, gently stir in the chopped mint, and serve.

PER SERVING: 308 CALORIES, 7.3G FAT, 1G SATURATED FAT, 7.9G TOTAL PROTEIN, 54MG CALCIUM, 110MG SODIUM

fusilli in lime and coconut milk sauce

This is a workable fusion, not confusion! I would have not dared make this dish without first using my Italian friends as guinea pigs. Great combination. If you are looking for a lower fat content, try diluting the coconut milk.

12oz (about 5–5½ cups) dried
   fusilli pasta
Salt, to taste
1 teaspoon grated lime zest
Cilantro leaves, for garnishing

For the sauce
1¼ cups coconut milk
1 lemongrass stalk,
   lightly crushed
1 fresh cilantro root,
   lightly crushed

2 kaffir lime leaves
⅔ cup water
1½ teaspoons sugar
⅜-inch piece of galangal,
   thinly sliced
2oz oyster mushrooms
4 small dried chilies,
   stems removed
1½ tablespoons freshly
   squeezed lime juice

Serves 3

Cook the fusilli in a large pot of boiling salted water, according to the package instructions, until tender but still firm to the bite.

Meanwhile, put the coconut milk in a saucepan over a high heat and bring to a boil. Add the lemongrass stalk, cilantro root, and lime leaves. Add the measured water, lower the heat, and simmer for 10 minutes. Strain to discard all the flavorings.

Season the sauce with salt to taste, and the sugar and stir well. Add the galangal, mushrooms, and dried chilies, then bring to a boil. Add the lime juice.

Remove from the heat, add the cooked drained fusilli, and stir to make sure that the pasta is well coated with the sauce. Transfer to individual serving plates, sprinkle with the lime zest, and garnish with cilantro leaves.

PER SERVING: 588 CALORIES, 18.7G FAT, 14.3G SATURATED FAT, 16G TOTAL
PROTEIN, 73MG CALCIUM, 590MG SODIUM

macaroni with roast cherry tomatoes

This is a little like macaroni & cheese, but without the cheese. It's so tasty that I don't think you will miss the cheese; however, if you must have some, you can add grated vegan cheese to the sauce.

1 cup cherry tomatoes
1 tablespoon olive oil
Salt and ground black pepper
8oz (about 2 cups) dried
　macaroni
3½ tablespoons vegan margarine
Heaping ¼ cup flour
2 cups vegetable broth
1 tablespoon Dijon mustard
2 eggs, beaten

Serves 4

Preheat the oven to 425°F. Place the cherry tomatoes in a 2-quart ovenproof dish. Drizzle the olive oil over them and season with salt and pepper. Roast the tomatoes for about 15 minutes, until they have softened slightly and the skins have split. Set aside.

Meanwhile, cook the macaroni in a large pot of boiling salted water according to the package instructions or until tender but firm to the bite. Drain and set aside.

Melt the margarine in a saucepan, add the flour, and cook for about 20 seconds. Slowly add the vegetable broth, stirring constantly until the sauce is smooth, and bring to a boil to thicken the sauce. Add the mustard and season with salt and pepper to taste. Allow to cool slightly.

Mix the eggs into the sauce and stir in well, then add the cooked macaroni. Return the pan to a low heat and stir well for about 5–6 minutes until the macaroni is heated through and the eggs are cooked—but take care not to scramble the eggs.

Transfer the pasta to the ovenproof dish containing the tomatoes and gently mix together. Bake in the oven for about 15–20 minutes until golden brown. Serve hot.

PER SERVING: 410 CALORIES, 18G FAT, 3.6G SATURATED FAT, 12.7G TOTAL PROTEIN, 71MG CALCIUM, 520MG SODIUM

fettuccine with oyster mushrooms and walnuts

This dish is so simple to prepare, yet the white wine and soy cream give it a touch of luxury. The resulting creamy sauce is just perfect for those ideal partners, mushrooms and walnuts.

3 tablepoons olive oil
8oz oyster mushrooms, torn into pieces
2 garlic cloves, crushed
1 onion, finely chopped
½ cup roughly chopped walnuts
⅔ cup dry white wine
¼ cup soy cream
2 tablepoons chopped rosemary leaves,
　plus 2 sprigs for garnishing
1 small leek, finely chopped
Salt, to taste
8oz dried fettuccine

Serves 4

Heat the oil in a frying pan and fry the mushrooms along with the garlic and onion until the mushrooms soften, then add the walnuts and fry, stirring, for another 3 minutes.

Pour in the wine and soy cream and add the chopped rosemary and leek. Simmer for a few minutes until the leek is tender. Season with salt to taste. Keep warm.

Meanwhile, cook the pasta in a large pot of boiling salted water, following the instruction on the package, until tender but firm to the bite. Drain well. Divide the pasta between serving bowls, top with the creamy sauce and garnish with the rosemary sprigs.

PER SERVING: 435 CALORIES, 20.9G FAT, 2.6G SATURATED FAT, 11.1G TOTAL PROTEIN, 84MG CALCIUM, 210MG SODIUM

vegetable lasagna

You can still enjoy a creamy lasagna even though you are committed to dairy-free eating. This vegetarian version uses soy milk and soy cheese, and tastes every bit as good as the usual sort, with just the right kind of texture.

9oz dried lasagna
2 tablespoons extra virgin olive oil
3 garlic cloves, crushed
1 red onion, finely chopped
1 eggplant, sliced crosswise, ¼-inch thick
1 red or yellow pepper, seeded and chopped
14½ oz can chopped tomatoes
1 zucchini, sliced crosswise, ⅜-inch thick
1 tablespoon tomato paste
1 cup vegetable broth
2oz (about ½ cup) soy cheese, finely grated
⅓ cup dry breadcrumbs

For the white sauce
3 tablespoons vegan margarine
3 tablespoons flour
2 cups plus 2 tablespoons soy milk
2 teaspoons Dijon mustard
Salt and pepper
2 tablespoons chopped fresh oregano

Serves 4

If using the type of dried lasagna sheets for which the instruction says "no need to precook", I still like to precook them as I then find it easier to arrange or tear them if I need to. Bring a large pot of lightly salted water to a boil, add the lasagne sheets, stir gently, and return to the boil. Boil for 10 minutes and drain well. Rinse the lasagne sheets with cold water to prevent them from sticking together. Set aside.

Heat the oil in a large pan over medium heat and fry the garlic and onion for a few minutes. Stir in the eggplant and red or yellow pepper, and sauté for another 10 minutes, stirring occasionally. Add the tomatoes, zucchini, tomato paste, and broth, cover, and let simmer for another 7–8 minutes until the vegetables are just tender — take care not to overcook. Remove from the heat and set aside.

Preheat the oven to 400°F.

To make the white sauce, melt the margarine in a pan, add the flour, and cook over medium heat for a couple of minutes, stirring constantly. Gently add the soy milk and mustard, then bring to a boil, continuing to stir well until the sauce thickens, Season with salt and pepper, to taste, and stir in the oregano.

Spread half of the vegetable mixture in a rectangular ovenproof dish, drizzle about 2–3 tablespoons of white sauce over it, and place a layer of lasagna sheets evenly on top. Repeat the process until you have used up all the vegetable mixture, making sure you end the process with white sauce on top of the last layer of lasagna sheets.

Mix together the soy cheese and breadcrumbs, and sprinkle evenly over the top of the dish. Bake in the oven for about 30–35 minutes until the top is golden brown. Serve hot.

PER SERVING: 524 CALORIES, 21.6G FAT, 3.3G SATURATED FAT, 18.3G TOTAL PROTEIN, 5G SOY PROTEIN, 158MG CALCIUM, 570MG SODIUM

steamed egg with scallions and shrimp

This is one of the healthiest ways to make an egg dish. It tastes like delicious soft white tofu and is very delicate and light in texture. It is also great made without shrimp if you are a vegetarian.

8 medium eggs
1 cup water
5½ oz (about 1–1¼ cups) cooked shrimp
2 tablespoons Thai fish sauce
2 teaspoons sugar
10 shallots, thinly sliced
4 scallions, finely chopped
Boiled rice (see page 49), for serving

To garnish
2 teaspoons crispy garlic (see page 75)
½ handful of cilantro leaves
Ground white pepper

Serves 4

Preheat a steamer on high until the water boils.

Beat the eggs with the water in a shallow bowl that will fit inside the top of the steamer, then stir in the shrimp, fish sauce, sugar, shallots, and scallions.

Put the bowl of egg mixture in the steamer, close the lid, and steam for 15–20 minutes, until the egg is set and firm.

Garnish with the crispy garlic, cilantro leaves, and a sprinkling of white pepper. Serve with boiled rice.

PER SERVING: 230 CALORIES, 13.5G FAT, 3.3G SATURATED FAT, 23.1G TOTAL PROTEIN, 193MG CALCIUM, 2,160MG SODIUM

tiger shrimp with celery and pine nuts

I adore pine nuts and believe they should be used more in all types of cooking. They have a unique flavor and character, especially when toasted. In this stir-fry recipe I have used them instead of the usual cashews or roasted peanuts.

2 tablespoons pine nuts
2 tablespoons vegetable oil
2 garlic cloves, crushed
9oz raw black tiger shrimp, peeled,
 deveined and de-headed; tails left on
¾ cup celery (preferably Chinese),
 chopped, including the leaves
2 tablespoons Thai fish sauce
1 tablespoon sugar
Ground white pepper
Cilantro leaves, for garnishing
Boiled rice (see page 49), or egg noodles, for serving

Serves 4

Toast the pine nuts in a dry frying pan without any oil until golden. Remove from the pan and set aside.

Heat the oil in a wok over medium heat. Add the garlic and stir for 30 seconds, taking care not to burn it, then add the shrimp and stir until they are half cooked.

Add the celery and continue to cook for 30–40 seconds. Season with the fish sauce, toasted pine nuts, and sugar, constantly stirring to blend in the seasoning well.

Sprinkle with ground white pepper and garnish with cilantro leaves. Serve hot with boiled rice or egg noodles.

PER SERVING: 163 CALORIES, 10.1G FAT, 1.1G SATURATED FAT, 13.2G TOTAL PROTEIN, 68MG CALCIUM, 710MG SODIUM

braised stuffed squid with spinach

Being a Thai person, I was born loving squid. Spinach is also a favorite of my son, Tim, so I use it quite a lot when cooking for him. I'm lucky that I have no problem getting Tim to eat greens!

1¼ lb (about 5 cups) potatoes,
 peeled and cut into slices
 ⅜-inch thick
1lb spinach, large stalks
 removed and leaves washed
2 tablespoons olive oil

Salt and pepper
8 medium squid tubes, cleaned
¼ cup vegan margarine,
 cut into small pieces
Hot chili powder, to taste
Juice of 2 lemons
Parsley, for garnishing

Serves 4

Cook the potatoes in a pan of boiling water for 10 minutes or until tender. Drain well and set aside.

Steam the spinach until very tender. Then drain well and let it cool a little. Squeeze the excess water from the steamed spinach with your hands. Put the spinach in a bowl, add the olive oil, mix well, and season with salt and pepper to your liking. Set aside.

Preheat the oven to 350°F and lightly oil a 2-quart round casserole dish.

Spoon the spinach loosely into the squid pouches, sealing the open end of each pouch with a wooden tooth pick. Set aside.

Arrange the potato slices, slightly overlapping, on the bottom of the casserole dish. Scatter half of the margarine over the potato slices. Arrange the stuffed squid tubes on top of the potato and scatter the rest of the margarine over the squid. Sprinkle with the hot chili powder, to taste, and more salt and pepper. Cover, and cook in the oven for about 35–40 minutes until the squid are tender.

When ready to serve, squeeze the juice from the lemons all over the squid and garnish with parsley.

PER SERVING: 415 CALORIES, 22.2G FAT, 3.8G SATURATED FAT, 25.8G TOTAL PROTEIN, 222MG CALCIUM, 540MG SODIUM

broiled sea bream (porgy) topped with ginger and fermented soybean sauce

I used to make this dish with pomfret (butterfish) but my Western customers found it too bony. After I substituted the pomfret with sea bream, I had no complaints!

2 tablespoons tapioca flour
¼ cup water
2 sea bream (porgy), 1lb, 10oz each, trimmed and gutted
2½ tablespoons vegetable oil
⅝-inch piece of fresh root ginger, peeled and finely sliced lengthways
4 garlic cloves, crushed
2 tablespoons fermented soybeans (black beans)
1 tablespoon light soy sauce

2 teaspoons Thai fish sauce
1½ tablespoons sugar
2½ cups straw mushrooms, drained and squeezed dry
6oz oyster mushrooms, trimmed
4 scallions, cut into 1-inch lengths
3½ cups chicken broth or water
1 tablespoon sesame oil

For garnishing
A few cilantro leaves
Ground white pepper

Serves 4

Put the flour in a small bowl and stir in the water to make a thin paste, then set aside. Make 3 slashes, about ⅛-inch deep, on each side of the sea bream, rub about 1 tablespoon of the oil all over the fish, and put them on a baking tray.

Preheat the broiler to medium and broil the fish for about 5–7 minutes on each side or until cooked. Keep warm.

Heat the remaining oil in a wok over medium heat. Add the ginger, garlic, and fermented soybeans, and stir-fry for about 30 seconds. Stir in the soy sauce, fish sauce, and sugar. Add all the mushrooms, scallions, and chicken broth or water, and stir together. Add the flour mixture and stir for about 30 seconds until the sauce thickens to a consistency that is slightly thinner than gravy. Finally, stir in the sesame oil.

Remove the fish carefully from the bone and place on individual serving plates. Spoon the sauce and vegetables over it and garnish with cilantro leaves and a sprinkling of pepper.

PER SERVING: 375 CALORIES, 15.1G FAT, 2.1G SATURATED FAT, 32.2G TOTAL PROTEIN, 2G SOY PROTEIN, 134MG CALCIUM, 1,210MG SODIUM

fish pie

You can use any fish of your choice for this. I have used haddock, cod, and salmon because they are all quite flaky and the color of the salmon is extremely appealing.

2½ lb potatoes, peeled, washed, and cubed
2¼ cups soy milk
13oz mixed haddock, cod, and salmon fillets
3½ tablespoons vegan margarine

4½ tablespoons flour
Salt and pepper
1¼ cups frozen peas
½ cup chopped fresh chives
1 teaspoon chopped fresh tarragon
2 tablespoons chopped parsley

Serves 4

Cook the potatoes in a pot of boiling salted water for 20 minutes until tender. Meanwhile, pour the soy milk into another saucepan and add the fish. Gently bring to a boil, then remove from the heat and let stand for about 5 minutes. Lift out the fish, using a slotted spoon, place it on a plate, and set aside. Measure about 1 cup of soy milk and reserve it for the mashed potato; keep the rest for the sauce.

To make the sauce, melt half the margarine in a heavy pan, and stir in the flour and cook for a minute. Slowly whisk in all but the 1 cup of soy milk to make the sauce, and bring to a boil. Stir and simmer for a few minutes.

Preheat the oven to 400°F. Drain the potatoes and mash them well. Stir in the cup of soy milk and remaining margarine, and season with salt and pepper to your liking. Add the peas to the sauce and heat gently for a couple of minutes without boiling. Stir in the chives and tarragon and immediately pour into a deep ovenproof dish. Flake in the fish, discarding any skin, and mix gently.

Spoon the mashed potato over the top to cover the filling and use a fork to rough up the surface. Place the dish on a baking sheet and bake in the oven for 30–35 minutes, until the potatoes are golden brown on top. Serve sprinkled with the parsley.

PER SERVING: 505 CALORIES, 17.9G FAT, 3.5G SATURATED FAT, 34.3G TOTAL PROTEIN, 3.8G SOY PROTEIN, 83MG CALCIUM, 320MG SODIUM

roast red snapper with chestnuts, raisins, and apple chunks

Red snapper is increasingly popular, and I have started to use it more in my cooking as it really is delicious. Baking a fish whole is a great way to keep it moist and succulent.

1 red snapper, weighing about
    3½lb, or 2 smaller
    ones, cleaned
Salt and pepper
2 tablespoons olive oil

For the sauce
3 tablespoons olive oil

1 onion, chopped
1⅓ cups cooked chestnuts
Handful of raisins
2 cooking apples, cored and
    cut into large chunks
2 red apples, cored and cut
    into large chunks
Juice of 1 orange

Serves 4

Preheat the oven to 400°F. Wash and pat dry the fish, then season with salt and pepper inside and out. Place in an oiled roasting pan and brush the skin with olive oil to keep it moist. Set aside while you make the sauce.

For the sauce, heat the olive oil in a pan and gently stir-fry the onion, chestnuts, raisins, and apple chunks for a few minutes. Gradually add the orange juice and cook over a low heat for another 2–3 minutes.

Spoon the sauce over and around the fish, then cover with foil and bake in the oven for about 30 minutes until the fish is cooked. To test if the fish is done, insert a knife into the thickest part and lift out a little of the flesh: if the flesh comes away easily from the bones and is opaque, the fish is cooked through. Otherwise, return it to the oven to cook a bit longer.

Carefully fillet the fish, transfer to individual serving plates, and spoon the sauce around it. Serve hot.

PER SERVING: 506 CALORIES, 18.3G FAT, 2.8G SATURATED FAT, 46.1G TOTAL PROTEIN, 132MG CALCIUM, 280MG SODIUM

steamed cod fillet with triple-flavor vegetables

This is a very healthy dish and, as its name indicates, is brimming with flavor. It's also very quick and easy to prepare. I really like the texture of cod when it is steamed.

4 cod fillets, each weighing about 7oz
¼ cup vegetable broth or water

For the sauce
1½ tablespoons vegetable oil
¼ cup carrot, cut into thin sticks
1½ oz (about 2–3) baby corn
½ cup onion, chopped
1⅓ oz (about ⅓–½ cup) pineapple, chopped
¼ cup tomato, chopped
⅓ cup mixed peppers, seeded and chopped
¾-inch slice of cucumber, quartered, seeded, and cut into thin sticks
1oz oyster mushrooms
1 tablespoon vegetable broth or water
2½ tablespoons Thai fish sauce
2 tablespoons tomato ketchup
1 tablespoon sugar
1 tablespoon distilled malt vinegar

Serves 4

Heat the water in a steamer to cook the fish. Put the fish on a plate, add the vegetable broth or water, and place in the top of the steamer for about 15–20 minutes or until it is cooked and opaque.

To make the sauce, heat the oil in a wok or large frying pan over medium heat. Add the carrot and baby corn and stir-fry for about 30 seconds, then add the onion, pineapple, tomato, peppers, cucumber, and oyster mushrooms, and stir-fry, constantly tossing and turning the ingredients.

Stir in the broth or water, season with the fish sauce, tomato ketchup, sugar, and vinegar, and continue stir-frying and tossing the ingredients until everything is hot and just tender. Do not overcook.

To serve, place the fish fillets on individual serving plates and top with the sauce.

PER SERVING: 247 CALORIES, 5.7G FAT, 0.8G SATURATED FAT, 38.9G TOTAL PROTEIN, 42MG CALCIUM, 1,000MG SODIUM

pan-fried monkfish with lemon and caper sauce

This is very simple and has a very strong but clean taste. What can I say—it's very me! Perfect for an informal dinner party, this goes well with some crisp salad greens.

3 tablespoons olive oil
1¼ lb monkfish tail, filleted, skinned and cut into 4 steaks
Ground black pepper
Mixed salad greens, for serving

For the sauce
3 tablespoons olive oil
4 shallots, chopped
1 tablespoon small capers, rinsed
4 canned anchovies in oil, drained and chopped
3 tablespoons dry white wine or water
3 tablespoons freshly squeezed lemon juice

Serves 4

Heat the oil in a large frying pan over medium heat and fry the monkfish steaks, using a spatula to press them against the pan. Once one side is slightly brown, turn the fish over and repeat, lowering the heat if necessary, until the fish steaks are cooked and brown on both sides. Remove from the pan and keep warm.

Heat the oil for the sauce over low heat and stir-fry the shallots until they release their fragrance, taking care not to burn them. Add the capers and anchovies and fry for 1 minute. Gradually pour in the wine or water and bring to a boil, then immediately remove from the heat and add the lemon juice.

Place the fish on individual serving plates and top with the sauce. Sprinkle with ground black pepper and serve with mixed salad greens.

PER SERVING: 332 CALORIES, 17.8G FAT, 2.7G SATURATED FAT, 40.3G TOTAL PROTEIN, 35MG CALCIUM, 260MG SODIUM

chicken with fresh peppercorns and slivered almonds

To roast dried chilies, simply toast in a dry frying pan for a couple of minutes over a low heat and keep tossing and turning them so they don't burn. When they release their aroma, they are ready.

1 cup flour
½ cup water
7oz (about 1 cup) skinless, boneless chicken breast, thinly sliced
Vegetable oil, for deep-frying
2 garlic cloves, pounded with 2 fresh cilantro roots to make a paste
3-inch piece of fresh ginger, peeled and finely cut into matchsticks
2 tablespoons Thai fish sauce

1½ tablespoons sugar
1 tablespoon fresh green peppercorns (see page 120)
⅓ cup slivered almonds
2 scallions, cut into ⅝-inch lengths
2 roasted dried chilies, chopped
¼ cup carrot, cut into matchsticks
½ cup mixed peppers, seeded and sliced
A few cilantro leaves, for garnishing

Serves 4

Put ⅔ cup flour in a bowl and add the water to make a smooth paste. Coat the chicken slices with the flour paste, then lift them up and let the excess paste drip off. Lightly sprinkle the slices with the remaining dry flour to hold the paste in place.

Heat enough oil for deep-frying in a wok over a high heat until it reaches 350°F. Deep-fry the chicken slices for 2–3 minutes until they are crisp and float to the surface. Remove from the oil and drain on paper towels. Keep warm. Heat 2 tablespoons of fresh vegetable oil in the wok over medium heat. Add the garlic, cilantro paste, and ginger, and stir-fry for about 15 seconds, taking care not to burn them. Season with the fish sauce and sugar. Add a splash of water if necessary.

Stir in the peppercorns, almonds, scallions, chilies, carrot, and mixed peppers. Add the chicken and continue stir-frying, constantly turning, until heated through. Transfer to a serving plate and garnish with cilantro leaves.

PER SERVING: 510 CALORIES, 31.2G FAT, 3.6G SATURATED FAT, 19.1G TOTAL PROTEIN, 102MG CALCIUM, 610MG SODIUM

baked poussins (squab chickens) with lemon and oregano

I like using lemon juice in many dishes. It really makes ordinary food taste better. People say that lemon juice is good only with seafood and chicken, but if you know how to use it properly it will go with almost any type of meat.

4 poussins (squab chickens)
3 tablespoons flour
2 tablespoons olive oil
1½ tablespoons grated lemon zest
1 onion, finely chopped
2 oregano sprigs, leaves only, finely chopped
1½ cups dry white wine
Salt and ground black pepper
Vegetables, for serving

Serves 4

Preheat the oven to 350°F.

Pat the poussins dry with paper towels, then dust with the flour to coat lightly all over. Set aside.

Heat the oil in a large heavy pan over medium heat. Stir in the lemon zest, onion, and oregano, and finally add the wine. Sauté until the onion turns tender and golden and the wine has half evaporated.

Place the poussins on a baking tray, pour half the sauce over them, and season to taste with salt and pepper. Bake in the oven for 35 minutes, turning once. When turning, pour the rest of the sauce over them to ensure that the poussins are not too dry.

Transfer the poussins to individual serving plates and spoon any sauce left in the baking tray over them. Serve with your preferred choice of vegetables, such as broccoli and carrots.

PER SERVING: 627 CALORIES, 38.1G FAT, 9.8G SATURATED FAT, 46G TOTAL PROTEIN, 52MG CALCIUM, 260MG SODIUM

chicken and vegetables with cashews and roasted dried chilies

I usually make either chicken with cashews and roasted dried chilies or the veggie version. The following recipe is the combination of both.

2 tablespoons vegetable oil
5½ oz (about ⅔–¾ cup) skinless boneless chicken breast, thinly sliced
10oz mixed seasonal vegetables of your choice (such as baby corn, broccoli, carrots, green beans and snow peas), prepared
¼ cup vegetable broth or water
1 tablespoons sugar
1½ tablespoons Thai fish sauce
Salt, to taste
1 teaspoon dark soy sauce
½ handful of cashews, roasted
3 large roasted dried chilies (see page 114), cut into small pieces with a pair of scissors
A few cilantro leaves, for garnishing
Boiled rice (see page 49), for serving

Serves 4

Heat the oil in a wok over medium heat. Add the chicken and stir-fry until almost cooked. Add the vegetables to the wok, starting with the ones that need the longest cooking time, and stir-fry, tossing and turning until they are half cooked. Stir in the broth or water, then reduce the heat.

Season with the sugar, fish sauce, salt to taste, and dark soy sauce, turn up the heat to high and continue stir-frying for a few seconds until all the vegetables are tender but still crisp. Stir in the cashews and dried chilies.

Transfer the chicken and vegetables to a serving plate and garnish with the cilantro leaves. This dish is great served with plain boiled rice.

PER SERVING: 165 CALORIES, 9.2G FAT, 1.1G SATURATED FAT, 12.6G TOTAL PROTEIN, 35MG CALCIUM, 680MG SODIUM

roast chicken with sage and balsamic vinegar

I like strong tastes in my food and I find balsamic vinegar has great character. This Western-style dish is so simple to make—you just need to remember to allow enough time for marinating the chicken to get the best flavor.

3½ tablespoons extra virgin olive oil
2 tablespoons balsamic vinegar
1 tablespoon chopped fresh sage
1 garlic clove, crushed
Ground black pepper
2 baby chickens, weighing about 18oz each, cut in half, backbone removed and flattened
Baked potatoes and dressed salad, for serving

Serves 4

Combine all the ingredients (except the chickens) to make a marinade. Place the chickens in a large dish and pour the marinade over them, rub in well, and cover the dish. Let them marinate for a couple of hours in the fridge.

Preheat the oven to 350°F.

Place the marinated chicken halves on a roasting rack set over a pan and roast for about 40–45 minutes, basting every so often, until cooked. Serve with baked potatoes and salad greens dressed with olive oil and balsamic vinegar.

PER SERVING: 402 CALORIES, 31.6G FAT, 7.2G SATURATED FAT, 27.9G TOTAL PROTEIN, 19MG CALCIUM, 110MG SODIUM

holy basil pork liver

I'm quite anemic and as liver is a good source of iron, my grandmother used to force me to eat a dish similar to this one. I hated it the first time but now I love it, especially when it is cooked with chili and holy basil. It is so tasty!

2 tablespoons vegetable oil
2 garlic cloves, pounded with
   1 fresh red chili to make a coarse paste
12oz (about 1½ cups) pork liver, sliced into bite-size pieces
1 cup onion, sliced
2 tablespoons Thai fish sauce
1½ teaspoons sugar
½ teaspoon dark soy sauce
3 tablespoons chicken broth or water
2 fresh red chilies, sliced lengthways
½ handful of holy basil leaves (if unavailable, use regular basil)
Boiled rice (see page 49), for serving

Serves 4

Heat the oil in a wok or a frying pan over medium heat. Add the garlic and chili paste and stir around for 10 seconds, taking care not to burn it.

Add the pork liver pieces and onion and continue stir-frying, constantly tossing and turning, for a few minutes. Season with the fish sauce, sugar, and soy sauce, and continue stirring to blend all the seasoning. Add the broth or water, followed by the chilies and holy basil leaves, and stir-fry for another 15 seconds.

Serve immediately with plain boiled rice.

PER SERVING: 176 CALORIES, 8.3G FAT, 1.5G SATURATED FAT, 20.4G TOTAL PROTEIN, 25MG CALCIUM, 710MG SODIUM

roast pork with rosemary

The pork makes its own tasty gravy as it cooks. Serve with boiled or steamed seasonal vegetables and, if you like, apple sauce on the side—the traditional Western accompaniment.

1 boned and rolled loin of pork, about 2¼ lb
Salt and coarsely ground black pepper
2 tablespoons olive oil
1 celery stick, chopped
1 onion, chopped
1 garlic clove, crushed
2 tablespoons chopped fresh rosemary,
   plus 2 whole rosemary sprigs
⅔ cup dry white wine
1 cup vegetable broth

Serves 5

Preheat the oven to 350ºF.

Rub the pork loin with salt and black pepper. Heat the olive oil in a flame- and ovenproof pan, add the pork, and brown well on all sides. Lift the pork out and set aside on a large plate.

Add the vegetables, garlic, and chopped rosemary to the pan and season with salt, to taste. Sauté for 5 minutes and place the meat on top. Turn up the heat, pour in the wine, and let it bubble rapidly for a minute, turning the pork over once. Then add half of the vegetable broth.

Cover the pan and cook in the oven for 1½ hours or until the pork is tender, turning the meat twice. If the vegetables seem to be drying out, add a little more broth. Lay the rosemary sprigs on top of the pork about 25 minutes before the end of the cooking time.

To serve, remove the rind from the pork and carve the meat into slices, then pour the sauce over it.

PER SERVING: 424 CALORIES, 27.3G FAT, 9.4G SATURATED FAT, 37G TOTAL PROTEIN, 48MG CALCIUM, 230MG SODIUM

roast duck red curry with pineapple and seedless grapes

In Thailand, the only curry we make using pre-cooked meat is roast duck curry, because we find that duck smells too strong to use in any of our cooking unless it is first roasted with spices.

5 kaffir lime leaves, torn
¼ cup ready-made
  Thai red curry paste
1 tablespoon vegetable oil
1 cup coconut milk
1 cup soy milk
9oz (about 1½–2 cups)
  roast duck fillets, sliced
  (skin removed)
½ handful of pineapple slices
  (if using canned, save the juice
  or syrup and use it instead of
  water, reducing the amount
  of sugar used accordingly)

3 tablespoons frozen peas
8 baby tomatoes
½ handful of seedless grapes
Scant cup water
¼ cup Thai fish sauce
1½ tablespoons sugar
Boiled rice (see page 49),
  for serving

For garnishing
1 fresh green chili,
  sliced lengthways
10–12 sweet basil leaves

Serves 4

Stir-fry the kaffir lime leaves and red curry paste with the oil in a wok or a saucepan, for about a minute, taking care not to burn the curry paste. Gently add the coconut and soy milk, stirring well, and let it simmer over a low heat for about 5–7 minutes or until oil starts to appear on the surface.

Add the roast duck, pineapple slices, peas, tomatoes, and grapes, along with the water, or juice from the pineapple (see above), and bring the curry to a boil. Lower the heat and season with the fish sauce and sugar. Give it one good stir, making sure the curry sauce covers all the ingredients, and simmer for 1 minute.

Garnish with the sliced chilies and sweet basil leaves and serve hot with plain boiled rice.

PER SERVING: 337 CALORIES, 23G FAT, 10.7G SATURATED FAT, 19.9G TOTAL PROTEIN, 1.7G SOY PROTEIN, 163MG CALCIUM, 1,590MG SODIUM

spare ribs with ginger sauce

Spare ribs are often found in barbecue joints and Chinese restaurants in the States. I like barbecue spare ribs, Western-style, but I think you can do more with them and here is an example.

2lb spare ribs,
  cut into 2-inch lengths
2 tablespoons vegetable oil
2 teaspoons fermented
  soybeans (black beans)
1–2 tablespoons water
8 dried jelly mushrooms (ear
  mushrooms), soaked in warm
  water until soft, drained, and
  squeezed dry
¾ cup onion, sliced

2 tablespoons Thai fish sauce
1½ tablespoons sugar
1 tablespoon distilled malt vinegar
1 teaspoon dark soy sauce
2¼-inch piece of fresh ginger,
  peeled and finely sliced
  lengthways
4 scallions, cut into 2-inch
  lengths
Ground white pepper
1 fresh red chili, thinly sliced
A few cilantro leaves

Serves 4

Cook the spare ribs in boiling water for about 5 minutes, then lower the heat to medium and continue to cook for another 10–15 minutes until the meat is tender and easily slides off the bone. Drain well and set aside.

Heat the oil over medium heat in a frying pan or a wok, add the fermented soybeans and stir around for about 10 seconds, taking care not to burn them. Add the cooked spare ribs and stir-fry, constantly tossing and turning, for about 1–2 minutes until the spare ribs absorb some of the sauce.

Add 1 tablespoon of water to keep the spare ribs moist and stir in the mushrooms and onion. Season with the fish sauce, sugar, vinegar, and soy sauce. Add the ginger and scallions, and continue stir-frying for about 15 seconds, when the dish should be ready. If it seems too dry, just add a little more water.

Transfer all the ingredients to a serving plate, sprinkle with ground white pepper, and garnish with red chili slices and cilantro leaves. Serve with plain boiled rice.

PER SERVING: 306 CALORIES, 19.4G FAT, 5.5G SATURATED FAT, 21.4G TOTAL PROTEIN, 2G SOY PROTEIN, 43MG CALCIUM, 860MG SODIUM

yellow curry with lamb and onions

This dish is influenced by Thailand's neighbor countries, such as Malaysia and Indonesia, together with the Thai population living in and around the south of Thailand where there is a huge Muslim population.

11oz lamb fillet (sirloin end of leg), cubed
¼ cup vegetable oil
4 tablespoons ready-made yellow curry paste
1 cup coconut milk
¾ cup soy milk
¾ cup water
4 potatoes, peeled and cut into chunks

1 large carrot, cut into chunks
1 large onion, quartered
2 tablespoons Thai fish sauce
1 tablespoon sugar
6 cardamom leaves
Salt and pepper
Nan bread, pita bread, or boiled rice (see page 49), for serving

Serves 4

Put the lamb in a saucepan, cover with water, bring to a boil, and simmer over medium heat until the meat is tender. Put the potato chunks in a different pot of boiling water and cook for 10 minutes until parboiled, then drain and set aside.

Heat the oil in another saucepan and stir-fry the yellow curry paste for a minute, taking care not to burn it. Add the coconut and soy milk, and bring to a boil. Drain the lamb cubes well and add to the curry sauce. Add the ¾ cup water, potatoes, carrot, and onion, and return to a boil. Reduce the heat to low and simmer for about 10 minutes to let the sauce penetrate the lamb.

Season with the fish sauce, sugar, and cardamom leaves, and continue to simmer until the potatoes are soft and tender. Adjust the seasoning to taste and remove from the heat. Serve hot with warm nan bread, pita bread, or boiled rice.

PER SERVING: 434 CALORIES, 26G FAT, 12.8G SATURATED FAT, 21.6G TOTAL PROTEIN, 1.5G SOY PROTEIN, 151MG CALCIUM, 940MG SODIUM

grilled lamb chops with fresh peppercorns, cilantro root, and shallots

If you cannot find fresh peppercorns then buy preserved peppercorns in brine, oil, or vinegar, and wash thoroughly before using. They will have the right soft texture.

1 tablespoon fresh green peppercorns
1 tablespoon chopped fresh cilantro root
1 tablespoon olive oil

Sea salt or kosher salt and ground black pepper
4 lamb chops (trimmed of fat)
1lb shallots, unpeeled
3 large potatoes, quartered
Scant ½ cup beef broth
2 tablespoons vegan margarine

Serves 4

Preheat the oven to 350°F. To make a marinade, in a large bowl mix together half of the green peppercorns, half of the chopped cilantro root, and the olive oil with salt and pepper to taste. Add the lamb chops and rub the marinade over each one to make sure they are coated. Cover and let marinate in the fridge for 20 minutes.

Meanwhile, place the shallots and potatoes in a roasting pan and bake in the oven for 45 minutes. Remove from the oven and let cool. Top and tail the shallots using a small knife and squeeze them out of their skins. Set aside with the potatoes.

Heat a lightly oiled grill pan or preheat the broiler to its highest setting and grill or broil the marinated lamb chops for 3–4 minutes on each side or to your liking.

While the chops are cooking, put the rest of the green peppercorns with the cooked shallots and potatoes in a saucepan, add the beef broth and place over a high heat until the broth has almost completely evaporated. Reduce the heat to medium and add the margarine, along with the rest of the chopped cilantro root. Season with salt and pepper and stir until the margarine has melted. Serve the grilled lamb chops with the vegetable mixture.

PER SERVING: 407 CALORIES, 19G FAT, 9.3G SATURATED FAT, 33.6G TOTAL PROTEIN, 71MG CALCIUM, 280MG SODIUM

beef stroganoff

When I was studying in the States, my guardian, Uncle Don, an American friend of my dad, used to make this dish for us every week. I loved it, and I've devised this recipe that replaces the usual sour cream with soy cream so that non-dairy eaters can enjoy it, too.

12oz round steak, cut into thick strips
Salt and ground black pepper
⅓ cup vegan margarine
1 large onion, cut in half and thinly sliced
8oz (about 3½–4 cups) button mushrooms
¼ cup brandy
Scant ½ cup beef or chicken broth
⅓ cup soy cream
⅓ cup soy milk
2 tablespoons grainy mustard
1 tablespoon chopped fresh tarragon
1 tablespoon chopped chives
Boiled rice (see page 49) or pasta, for serving

Serves 4

Toss the steak strips in black pepper. Heat 3 tablespoons of the margarine in a heavy frying pan until hot and sizzling. Cook the steak strips, in batches, for a couple of minutes. Remove from the pan and keep warm.

Heat the remaining margarine in the pan and cook the onion and mushrooms for a few minutes. Add the brandy, broth, and soy cream and soy milk, and let simmer until the sauce thickens. Stir in the mustard and tarragon and season with salt and black pepper.

Put the beef into the sauce and heat, stirring, until the meat is hot. Sprinkle with the chopped chives and serve with boiled rice or pasta.

PER SERVING: 389 CALORIES, 28.9G FAT, 7.6G SATURATED FAT, 21.6G TOTAL PROTEIN, 0.5G SOY PROTEIN, 79MG CALCIUM, 470MG SODIUM

spicy linguine with ground beef and basil

The Italians use so many similar herbs and ingredients to the Thais in their cooking and this dish is one very good example. It reminds me of a spaghetti ragù but spicier and without tomatoes. A winning formula!

12oz dried linguine
Salt and pepper

For the sauce
2 tablespoons extra virgin olive oil
1 garlic clove, pounded with 1 fresh red chili to make a coarse paste
7oz lean ground beef
¾ cup onion, finely chopped
1½ tablespoons Thai fish sauce
1 tablespoon sugar
½ teaspoon dark soy sauce
2½ tablespoons water
1 fresh chili, sliced lengthways
10 holy basil leaves (or regular basil)

Serves 2–3

Cook the linguine in a large pot of boiling salted water, according to the package instructions, until tender but firm to the bite.

Meanwhile, make the sauce. Heat the oil in a frying pan over medium heat. Add the garlic and chili paste, and stir around for 10 seconds. Add the beef and continue stir-frying, constantly tossing and turning, for about 2 minutes until it is half cooked.

Add the onion and stir-fry for another 20 seconds, then season with the fish sauce, sugar, and soy sauce, and continue stirring. Add the water, then stir in most of the chili and most of the holy basil leaves, and stir-fry for another 15–20 seconds.

Add the cooked drained pasta to the sauce and mix in well. Transfer the pasta with the sauce to individual serving plates. Garnish with the remaining chili and holy basil.

PER SERVING (FOR 3): 628 CALORIES, 15.9G FAT, 4.1G SATURATED FAT, 30.2G TOTAL PROTEIN, 53MG CALCIUM, 840MG SODIUM

beef stew with onions and yorkshire puddings

This is a very cozy and homey type of dish. It is especially delicious served with Yorkshire puddings!

18oz stewing beef, cubed
3¼ cups beef broth
2 thyme sprigs
Salt and ground black pepper
14oz (about 2) large onions, quartered
1½ tablespoons brown sugar
2 tablespoons flour
14oz small baking potatoes, peeled
14oz (about 2¾–3¼ cups) carrots, cut into chunks

Serves 4

Put the beef in a heavy pan with the broth, and thyme sprigs. Season with salt and pepper and bring to a boil. Lower the heat and simmer for 30 minutes.

Add the onions to the pan, stir in the sugar, and simmer for another 20 minutes.

Meanwhile, preheat the oven to 350°F.

Mix the flour with a little water to make a runny paste, pour into the pan, and stir in well to thicken. Transfer the contents of the pan to an ovenproof dish, stir in the potatoes and carrots, and cover with the lid. Cook in the oven for at least 1 hour, until the beef is tender. Remove from the oven and keep warm while you cook the Yorkshire puddings.

PER SERVING (WITHOUT YORKSHIRE PUDDINGS): 382 CALORIES, 8.9G FAT, 3.5G SATURATED FAT, 33.2G TOTAL PROTEIN, 104MG CALCIUM, 460MG SODIUM

yorkshire puddings

Since my boarding-school years I have always loved Yorkshire pudding with gravy. These soy milk versions taste just the same as the regular ones.

⅔ cup minus 1 tablespoon all-purpose flour
Salt and pepper
1 medium egg, beaten
½ cup soy milk
2–3 tablespoons olive oil

Raise the temperature of the oven to 425°F. Put the flour in a mixing bowl, and add a pinch of salt and pepper. Add the beaten egg in the middle of the flour and slowly whisk in the soy milk, working from the center outwards, until all the flour is incorporated.

Put some oil into 8 holes of a shallow muffin pan and place it in the oven for about 5 minutes until the oil is very hot and sizzling. Divide the batter between 8 holes of the tin and bake in the oven for 15–20 minutes until well risen and crisp on top.

Serve with the beef, vegetables, and gravy.

PER SERVING (YORKSHIRE PUDDINGS ONLY): 145 CALORIES, 7.7G FAT, 1.2G SATURATED FAT, 4.2G TOTAL PROTEIN, 1G SOY PROTEIN, 40MG CALCIUM, 120MG SODIUM

5

desserts and drinks

asian fruit salad

This is extremely refreshing and a wonderful dessert to follow a spicy and heavy main course. It is also lovely to have with crushed ice on a hot summer's day. If fresh jackfruit and palm fruit are unavailable, substitute canned, but discard the syrup.

2½ cups orange juice
2 tablespoons sugar
1 tablespoon freshly squeezed lime juice
1 ripe but firm mango, peeled and cut into small cubes
1 ripe but firm papaya, peeled and cut into small cubes
4 pieces of jackfruit, torn into strips
4 palm fruits, cut into strips
¼ small pineapple, peeled, cored, and cut into bite-size pieces

Serves 4

Put the orange juice in a pitcher and stir in the sugar. Add the lime juice and stir well. Set aside.

Place all the fruits in a large glass bowl. Pour in the prepared juice, cover with plastic wrap and refrigerate.

Serve chilled, by itself, or with any fruit sorbet.

PER SERVING: 239 CALORIES, 0.6G FAT, 0G SATURATED FAT, 2.8G TOTAL PROTEIN, 66MG CALCIUM, 20MG SODIUM

crispy fresh mango with cinnamon and berry sauce

The chilled berry sauce goes extremely well with the warm crispy mango slices. It was certainly a hit with the customers at my restaurant.

Vegetable oil, for deep-frying
2 ripe but firm mangoes, peeled and sliced lengthways into strips ⅜-inch wide
A heaping ¾ cup flour

For the sauce
1¼–1⅓ cups mixed berries (such as raspberries, blueberries, and strawberries)
1½ tablespoons sugar
Scant ½ cup cranberry juice
Juice of 1 lime

To garnish
½ handful of mixed berries
4 mint sprigs
Ground cinnamon

Serves 4

First make the sauce by putting all the ingredients in a blender and blending until smooth. Refrigerate.

Heat enough oil for deep-frying in a wok to 350°F. Lightly coat the mango strips with the flour and slide them one by one into the hot oil. Fry until they are lightly browned and crisp, gently turning them over once or twice to make sure they are cooked evenly on both sides.

Remove from the hot oil using a slotted spoon or a pair of tongs and drain well on paper towels.

Arrange the crispy fried mango slices on serving plates. Garnish each plate with berries and a sprig of mint, and sprinkle them with ground cinnamon. Serve the chilled berry sauce in a bowl.

PER SERVING: 365 CALORIES, 15.8G FAT, 1.8G SATURATED FAT, 4.1G TOTAL PROTEIN, 82MG CALCIUM, 10MG SODIUM

pan-fried fresh pineapple and toasted coconut

Instead of the usual banana in caramel sauce, why not try this caramelized pineapple? You can adapt this recipe by drizzling the pan-fried pineapple with honey instead of brown sugar, if you wish.

1 tablespoon dried shredded coconut
1 medium pineapple, peeled, cored, and cut in half lengthways
2 tablespoons vegan margarine
¼ cup light brown sugar
¼ cup freshly squeezed lime juice
Lime wedges, for decorating
Dairy-free coconut or vanilla ice cream, for serving

Serves 4

Dry-fry the desiccated coconut in a frying pan over a very low heat, constantly stirring to prevent burning, until it is lightly browned. Set aside.

Cut the pineapple flesh lengthways into ½-inch wedges and set aside.

Meanwhile, heat half of the vegan margarine in a large frying pan over a low heat. Slide about 4 of the pineapple wedges into the pan and cook on each side for a few minutes or until they turn slightly golden.

Sprinkle half of the sugar all over the pineapple wedges followed by half of the lime juice. Continue to stir constantly to make sure the sugar melts. Turn over the pineapple wedges once. Remove from the pan and keep warm while you fry the remaining pineapple wedges in the same way.

Transfer the caramelized pineapple to a large serving plate and sprinkle with the toasted coconut. Decorate with lime wedges and serve with dairy-free coconut or vanilla ice cream.

PER SERVING (WITHOUT ICE CREAM): 205 KCALS, 8.4G FAT, 2.9G SATURATED FAT, 1G TOTAL PROTEIN, 45MG CALCIUM, 0.06G SODIUM

peaches with meringue and chopped almonds

Peaches are one of my favorite fruits—they are juicy and succulent. This dessert is very light yet satisfying, with so many blends of different flavors and textures.

2 tablespoons vegan margarine
4 large peaches, cut in half
1 tablespoon chopped almonds
1 egg white
3 tablespoons superfine sugar

Serves 4

Preheat the oven to 400°F. In the oven, melt the margarine in a small roasting pan, then place the peach halves in the pan and scatter in the almonds. Roast for 20 minutes, turning from time to time until the peaches are tender.

Meanwhile, beat the egg white in a mixing bowl to stiff peaks, then gradually beat in the sugar to make a firm and glossy meringue.

Turn the peaches cut side up in the roasting pan and spoon some meringue on top of each one. Return to the oven for another 5 minutes or until the meringue is lightly browned. Serve the meringue-topped peaches hot, along with their juice and the nuts from the roasting pan.

PER SERVING: 170 CALORIES, 8.4G FAT, 1.4G SATURATED FAT, 3.2G TOTAL PROTEIN, 26MG CALCIUM, 80MG SODIUM

baked apples with walnuts and custard

When one of my restaurant staff was returning to Thailand, I organized a farewell party for her and she begged me to make Western dishes. This apple dessert was one of the dishes I whipped up.

2 Granny Smith apples,
  cored but not peeled
2 Red Delicious apples,
  cored but not peeled
¼ cup walnut pieces
¼ cup golden raisins
2 tablespoons brown sugar
2 tablespoons honey
4 teaspoons vegan margarine,
  plus extra for greasing

For the custard
1¼ cups soy milk
½ tablespoon instant vanilla
  pudding
1 egg yolk
½ teaspoon vanilla extract
Sugar, to taste

Serves 4

Preheat the oven to 375°F. Grease a baking pan large enough to hold all 4 apples.

Enlarge the core opening at the stem end of each apple to about an inch in diameter by cutting at an angle with a small knife. Arrange the apples stem-end up in the prepared pan. Fill them with a mixture of walnut pieces and golden raisins, sprinkle with brown sugar, and drizzle with honey. Top each with a teaspoon of the margarine and bake in the oven for 45 minutes.

Meanwhile, make the custard. Warm most of the soy milk in a saucepan over medium heat (reserve 1 tablespoon) but do not let it boil. In a bowl, mix the vanilla pudding powder with the reserved soy milk until smooth. Blend in the egg yolk and vanilla extract and pour the warm soy milk over the custard mixture, whisking constantly. Return the mixture to the saucepan and stir over a low heat until it thickens. Sweeten with sugar to taste. Serve the apples hot with the soy milk custard.

PER SERVING: 287 CALORIES, 12.2G FAT, 2G SATURATED FAT, 4.4G TOTAL PROTEIN, 2G SOY PROTEIN, 39MG CALCIUM, 70MG SODIUM

pear crumble

You can make a scrumptious dairy-free crumble topping for this classic Western dessert, and the fruit is precooked using vegan margarine to give it a luxurious texture. It is delicious with dairy-free custard (see the recipe to the left).

1 tablespoon plus 2 teaspoons vegan margarine
6 ripe but firm pears, peeled, cored, and chopped
¼ cup caster sugar
Dairy-free custard (see left), for serving

For the crumble topping
⅓ cup vegan margarine
½ cup sugar
Heaped ¾ cup flour

Serves 4

Preheat the oven to 350°F.

Melt the margarine in a pan, add the chopped pears, and cook over a high heat, constantly stirring and turning, until the fruit is soft and most of the liquid has evaporated.

Add the sugar and stir in well to make sure it is completely dissolved. Remove from the heat and transfer the fruit and syrup to a baking dish.

To make the topping, put all the ingredients in a bowl and rub them between your fingers until the mixture resembles breadcrumbs.

Spread the crumble mixture evenly over the pears and bake for 25–30 minutes or until the top is golden brown. Serve the pear crumble hot with custard.

PER SERVING: 581 CALORIES, 22.2G FAT, 4.5G SATURATED FAT, 4.6G TOTAL PROTEIN, 2G SOY PROTEIN, 88MG CALCIUM, 220MG SODIUM

black sticky rice pudding with young coconut flesh

Most Thai puddings and desserts use coconut milk or cream as a main ingredient where Western desserts would use dairy products. This makes a great alternative to the traditional rice pudding.

¼ teaspoon salt
⅓ cup coconut cream
1½ cups black short-grain rice
2½ cups water
1 cup sugar
4½ oz (about 1¾–2¼ cups)
  young coconut flesh, cut into strips

Serves 4

Mix the salt and coconut cream together in a pan over a very low heat, stirring constantly to prevent the cream from separating. Remove from the heat as soon as the salt has dissolved and set aside.

Wash the rice twice, place in a pan, and add the water. Place over medium heat and boil until the rice is cooked through. The grains will split when they are cooked. Add the sugar and continue to boil and gently stir until it has totally dissolved.

Spoon the sticky rice pudding into individual serving bowls and top each portion with a few coconut strips and a spoonful of the coconut cream. When ready to eat, stir both the coconut strips and the coconut cream into the pudding.

PER SERVING: 546 CALORIES, 9.2G FAT, 6.7G SATURATED FAT, 6.9G TOTAL PROTEIN, 15MG CALCIUM, 160MG SODIUM

bananas in coconut milk with corn

A very comforting dessert—you'll love the creamy coconut sauce. Pandanus leaves, also called screwpine leaves, are available from Thai grocery stores but if you can't find one, simply omit, as the toasted sesame seeds provide plenty of flavor.

2 teaspoons sesame seeds
1¾ cups coconut milk
Scant cup water
1 pandanus leaf, cleaned, wiped dry,
  and tied into a knot (optional)
½ cup sugar
½ teaspoon salt
¼ cup fresh or drained canned corn
4 ripe but firm medium bananas, peeled, cut in half
  lengthways, and each half cut into 6–8 pieces

Serves 4

Dry-fry the sesame seeds in a frying pan over a low heat until they release their aroma and turn golden brown. Remove from the pan and set aside.

Put the coconut milk and water in a saucepan over medium heat and bring to a boil. Add the knotted pandanus leaf (if using) and simmer for a few minutes. Stir in the sugar and salt. If using fresh corn, add it now and cook for another minute or so.

Add the banana pieces and, if you are using it, the canned corn and simmer for about 1½ minutes until the banana pieces are tender but not too soft. Discard the pandanus leaf.

Spoon the bananas and coconut milk into individual serving bowls. Sprinkle with the toasted sesame seeds and serve warm.

PER SERVING: 383 CALORIES, 18.2G FAT, 14.3G SATURATED FAT, 3.6G TOTAL PROTEIN, 55MG CALCIUM, 350MG SODIUM

coconut flans (crème caramels)

Another traditional Western dessert which has been given a new twist with dairy-free ingredients. Here, coconut milk replaces the usual cow's milk with superb results. This also makes a fabulous dinner party dessert.

¾ cup sugar
1¾ cups coconut milk
3 eggs
A few drops of vanilla extract

Serves 6

Preheat the oven to 300°F.

Put 5 tablespoons of the sugar in a heavy pan over a low heat. Stir until the sugar has melted and then continue heating until it turns golden brown, watching it like a hawk so that it does not burn. Quickly pour equal amounts of the caramelized sugar into 4 custard cups and place them in a roasting pan.

Heat the coconut milk in a saucepan over a low heat until warm but do not boil. Beat the eggs in a bowl with the remaining sugar until the texture is light and creamy. Gradually add the warm coconut milk, constantly beating the mixture, and then add the vanilla.

Strain the custard mixture into a large measuring cup and pour an equal amount into each custard cup. Carefully pour hot water into the roasting pan to come halfway up the outside of the custard cups. Place the pan in the oven and bake for 35-40 minutes, until the custards are set. Let cool and refrigerate.

When ready to eat, run a knife around the edge of each flan and invert onto individual serving plates.

PER SERVING: 262 CALORIES, 14.2G FAT, 10.2G SATURATED FAT, 4.7G TOTAL PROTEIN, 39MG CALCIUM, 170MG SODIUM

lemon cheesecake with strawberries

I actually prefer this cheesecake to the usual dairy-laden recipe. It tastes much lighter and fresher. Thanks to my friend Noi who helped me with this recipe at the expense of her husband's birthday cake!

3⅓ tablespoons vegan margarine
¼ cup sugar
1¾ cups crushed graham crackers

For the filling
Juice and grated zest of 1 lemon
¼ cup water
1 tablespoon gelatin, or a vegetarian alternative
  such as agar or carrageen
1 cup vegan quark or other dairy-free soft cheese
⅔ cup soy milk
⅓ cup plus 1 tablespoon sugar
3 tablespoons dairy-free lemon curd, for the topping
Fresh strawberries, for decorating

Serves 6

Melt the vegan margarine and sugar over a gentle heat. Stir in the crushed crackers and mix well. Press into the bottom of an 8-inch round springform cake pan in an even layer and chill in the fridge.

To make the filling, put the lemon juice and zest, water, and gelatin in the top of a double broiler set over hot water and stir until the gelatin has dissolved. Let cool. Soften the quark in a large mixing bowl, mix in the soy milk and sugar, and beat until blended. Add the gelatin mixture and stir well. Spoon onto the graham cracker crust and chill for 3-4 hours until set.

Remove the collar from the pan and place the cheesecake on a serving plate. Spread the top with the lemon curd and decorate with fresh strawberries.

PER SERVING: 349 CALORIES, 13.7G FAT, 3.3G SATURATED FAT, 9.6G TOTAL PROTEIN, 0.6G SOY PROTEIN, 107MG CALCIUM, 240MG SODIUM

chocolate brownies with banana and chunky chestnuts

Cooked chestnuts are quite expensive, but I recommend that you buy good-quality ones which are firm and chunky, rather than the cheaper flaky and soft ones.

6oz (about 1 cup) luxury dark chocolate (at least 75 percent cocoa)
¾ cup vegan margarine, plus extra for greasing
2 very ripe medium bananas, peeled
2 medium eggs
1 cup minus 1½ tablespoons all-purpose flour
½ teaspoon baking powder

1 cup plus 1½ tablespoons sugar
½ teaspoon salt
1¼ cups canned or vacuum-packed cooked whole chestnuts

For the chocolate sauce
3½ oz (about ½–⅔ cups luxury dark chocolate (at least 75 percent cocoa)
1¾ cups vegan margarine

Serves 8–12

Preheat the oven to 325°F. Break up the chocolate into the top of a double broiler and add the margarine. Set it over gently simmering water and melt, stirring occasionally. (You will also use this method to make the chocolate sauce; see below.)

Mash the bananas in a large mixing bowl. Beat the eggs into the bananas until the whites and yolks are well blended. Add the flour, baking powder, sugar, and salt, then immediately add the warm chocolate mixture and gently fold in.

Add most of the chestnuts to the batter and gently fold in. Pour the batter into a greased nonstick 8-inch-square cake pan, and ensure that the chestnuts are evenly distributed. Use the reserved chestnuts to fill any gaps and make sure that all the chestnuts are covered with the batter. Bake on the middle shelf of the oven for 25–30 minutes until the mixture is set. Let cool in the pan for 10–15 minutes before cutting into squares for serving.

To make the chocolate sauce, follow the method in the first paragraph. Serve the brownies with the hot chocolate sauce.

PER SERVING (FOR 12): 383 CALORIES, 24.5G FAT, 7.9G SATURATED FAT, 4.3G TOTAL PROTEIN, 40MG CALCIUM, 250MG SODIUM

coffee-flavored cake

My friend Noi makes cakes for a living and she created this cake at my request. It works beautifully and is so decadent—it is definitely a very grown-up kind of cake!

¾ cup plus 1½ tablespoons all-purpose flour
2 teaspoons baking powder
Pinch of salt
½ cup plus 1 tablespoon sugar
4 large eggs, separated
¾ cup peanut oil
¾ cup water
1 teaspoon coffee essence
½ teaspoon crème fraiche

For the coffee cream frosting
½ cup vegan margarine
1½ cups confectioners' sugar
1 teaspoon instant coffee powder, mixed with 1 teaspoon hot water and left to cool
Pinch of instant coffee, for decorating

Serves 6–8

Preheat the oven to 325°F. Mix together the flour, baking powder, salt, and half of the sugar in a large bowl, and make a well in the center. Mix the egg yolks, oil, water, and coffee extract together, drop into the well, and blend into the dry ingredients. Set aside.

Beat the egg whites and crème fraiche in a separate bowl into soft peaks and gradually beat in the remaining sugar until stiff. Fold the egg-white mixture into the flour mixture and blend well together. Spoon the batter into an ungreased 8-inch round cake pan and bake in the oven for 40 minutes or until well risen and springy to the touch. Turn the cake out of the pan and let cool on a wire rack.

To make the coffee cream frosting, beat the vegan margarine until smooth and gradually beat in the confectioners' sugar. Finally beat in the coffee mixture.

Cut the cooled cake in half horizontally and spread half of the frosting on the lower half of the cake. Place the top half of the cake back in position over the frosting. Spread the rest of the icing on top of the cake and sprinkle with a pinch of instant coffee.

PER SERVING (FOR 8): 492 CALORIES, 32.1G FAT, 6.4G SATURATED FAT, 5.2G TOTAL PROTEIN, 82.5MG CALCIUM, 410MG SODIUM

mung beans in sugar syrup

I love this dessert. It is one of the very few Thai desserts that does not contain coconut milk. Rather than eating it as a dessert, I personally prefer to have it as a snack during the day, perhaps instead of tea and cookies. A much healthier choice.

1 cup mung beans
5 cups water
¾ cup plus 2 tablespoons brown sugar

Serves 4–6

Pick out and discard all the colored and misshapen beans. Wash the beans, cover with warm water, and let soak for 2–3 hours or, even better, overnight. Wash again and drain before use.

Pour the measured water into a pan and bring to a boil. Add the mung beans and cook over medium heat for 30–45 minutes until tender and cooked through. The beans will split open once they are cooked.

Add the brown sugar and stir until it has dissolved. Return to a boil, then remove from the heat.

Serve cold or hot; I personally prefer it hot.

PER SERVING: 371 CALORIES, 0.6G FAT, 0.1G SATURATED FAT, 13.5G TOTAL PROTEIN, 82MG CALCIUM, 20MG SODIUM

candied yuca with soy cream

Yuca (pronounced YOO-ka, and not to be confused with the yucca plant, which is a different plant entirely), is also called cassava and manioc, and you should be able to find this long brown-skinned root in Caribbean and Latin American markets.

1½ cups sugar
2 cups water
1½ lb yuca, peeled, cut in half lengthways
    and then cut across into 3-inch pieces

For the topping
⅔ cup soy cream
Pinch of salt

Serves 4

To make the topping, put the soy cream and salt in a small pan and warm over a low heat. Stir constantly to make sure that the salt dissolves completely. Set aside.

Put the sugar and water in a stainless steel wok or large pan and heat over medium heat. (Cooked Thai desserts are usually made in a brass wok, which does not discolor the ingredients.) Gently stir to make sure the sugar is fully dissolved and bring the mixture to a boil.

Reduce the heat, add the yuca pieces, and make sure that they are totally covered with the syrup. Let simmer for 20–30 minutes or until the yuca is cooked through and has absorbed almost all of the syrup, turning occasionally to make sure the syrup is well distributed among the yuca pieces.

Remove from the heat and transfer to individual serving plates or bowls. Drizzle with the lightly salted soy cream before serving.

PER SERVING: 611 CALORIES, 7G FAT, 1G SATURATED FAT, 2.2G TOTAL PROTEIN, 73MG CALCIUM, 130MG SODIUM

watermelon ice

Instead of following the recipe below, if you are in a hurry you can make a lovely frozen drink by blending the watermelon flesh with sugar syrup, to taste, and some ice cubes, along with a small quantity of lime juice and it should give you the same satisfaction.

½ cup sugar
½ cup water
18oz (about 2½ cups) watermelon, plus 4 watermelon
    wedges with the rind left on, for serving
2 tablespoons freshly squeezed lemon juice

Serves 4

Put the sugar and water into a pan and heat gently until the sugar has dissolved. Pour into a large bowl and let cool.

Cut the watermelon into wedges and remove the flesh from the rind, discarding the seeds. Cut the flesh into small pieces. Put the watermelon pieces into a blender and blend until smooth.

Add the cooled sugar syrup and lemon juice to the watermelon slush in the blender and gently blend for a few seconds.

Transfer the mixture into a freezer container and freeze for about 1½ hours. Remove from the freezer and beat the mixture, then freeze for another 2 hours, beating the mixture at 30-minutes intervals until it has frozen firm.

Transfer the watermelon ice from the freezer to the fridge 20 minutes before it is to be served. Serve in scoops, accompanying each portion with a fresh watermelon wedge.

PER SERVING: 138 CALORIES, 0.4G FAT, 0G SATURATED FAT, 0.6G TOTAL PROTEIN, 12MG CALCIUM, 10MG SODIUM

orange soy yogurt ice cream

People on a dairy-free diet who just can't live without ice cream will be delighted to find that this recipe, made with soy cream instead of heavy cream, works extremely well. It can also be made with lemon or lime juice instead of the orange juice.

⅓ cup plus 1 tablespoon freshly squeezed orange juice
2 cups plus 2 tablespoons soy yogurt
⅔ cup soy cream
½ cup sugar
Thin strips of orange zest, for decorating

Serves 6

Put the orange juice into a bowl, add the yogurt, cream, and sugar, and mix well. Then churn the mixture in an ice cream maker, following the manufacturer's instructions.

If you do not have an ice cream maker, freeze the mixture in a freezeproof container for 1–2 hours or until it begins to set around the edges. Turn the mixture out into a bowl and stir with a fork or beat in a food processor until smooth. Return to the freezer and freeze for another 2–3 hours, or until firm. Cover the container with a lid for storing.

Serve the ice cream in scoops, decorated with strips of the orange zest.

PER SERVING: 175 CALORIES, 7.9G FAT, 0.6G SATURATED FAT, 5G TOTAL PROTEIN, 4.2G SOY PROTEIN, 27MG CALCIUM, 10MG SODIUM

chilled cappuccino cups

I was asked to provide a recipe for cappuccino or coffee with soy milk. Well, here is a sophisticated one for you to try. Those who like whipped cream can whip soy cream and put it on top of this chilled coffee pudding before sprinkling with dark chocolate powder.

1¼ cups soy milk
2 tablespoons instant coffee
1 egg and 3 egg yolks
Scant ⅔ cup superfine sugar

For decorating
Dark chocolate powder
4 mint sprigs

Serves 4

Preheat the oven to 350°F.

Heat the soy milk with the instant coffee. Beat the egg and egg yolks with the sugar until well blended. Pour the hot soy milk mixture over the eggs and sugar, constantly beating.

Place 4 ovenproof coffee cups in a roasting pan. Pour the mixture into the cups. Very carefully pour enough hot water into the pan to come halfway up the outside of the cups. Put the pan in the oven and bake for 30 minutes or until the custards are just set. Remove the cups from the oven, let cool, then chill in the fridge for about 1½ hours.

Serve sprinkled with dark chocolate powder and decorated with mint sprigs.

PER SERVING: 245 CALORIES, 9G FAT, 2.7G SATURATED FAT, 7.2G TOTAL PROTEIN, 2.2G SOY PROTEIN, 52MG CALCIUM, 50MG SODIUM

mango smoothie

To make a tasty smoothie, you must use at least one fruit that has a dense texture, such as a banana or guava, to thicken the drink so that you can avoid using yogurt or cream. You can also substitute the brown sugar with honey.

2½ cups chilled soy milk
Scant cup chilled mango juice
2 tablespoons brown sugar
2 ripe mangoes, pitted, chopped and frozen
2 bananas, sliced and frozen

Serves 4

Put the soy milk, mango juice, and sugar into a blender and blend on a slow setting until well combined. Add the mango and banana chunks and blend until smooth.

PER SERVING: 220 CALORIES, 3G FAT, 0.3G SATURATED FAT, 5.3G TOTAL PROTEIN, 4.3G SOY PROTEIN, 46MG CALCIUM, 50MG SODIUM

lemongrass hot drink

If you don't like lemongrass, then try making the drink with ginger, but omit the citrus.

3¼ cups water
4 lemongrass stalks, lightly crushed
3 tablespoons light brown sugar or honey (optional)

Serves 4

Bring the water to a boil in a small saucepan over medium heat. Add the lemongrass, reduce the heat, and let simmer for 7–8 minutes or until the water begins to turn yellow. Remove the lemongrass stalks and add the sugar or honey, stirring until dissolved. Serve the drink hot by itself or with cookies.

PER SERVING (WITH SUGAR/HONEY): 35 CALORIES, 0G FAT, 0G SATURATED FAT, 0.1G TOTAL PROTEIN, 2MG CALCIUM, 10MG SODIUM

resources

The various dietetic nutrition societies are a good option for getting information about lactose intolerance as well as allergy, as they will be able to put you in touch with local groups, and inform you about up-and-coming events. They also increase awareness within the food industry and lead research into food intolerance. For those with an allergy or anaphalyxis to cow's milk and its derivatives, finding information on the issues and risks concerning cross-contamination, food preparation, and eating out is essential. This information is also covered in other publications and in fact-sheets from allergy specialists, and support associations such as The Food Allergy & Anaphylaxis Network.For anyone looking to exclude dairy from their diet completely for whatever reason you should get an appointment to see a registered dietitian or nutritionist to ensure that you do not miss out on any vital nutrients.

Dietetic and Nutrition Societies and Information Services

USA
American Dietetic Association
Headquarters, 120 South Riverside Plaza,
Suite 2000, Chicago, IL 60606-6995
Tel: 1-800-877-1600
www.eatright.org

American Heart Association
National Center
7272 Greenville Avenue
Dallas, TX 75231
Tel: 1-800-AHA-USA-1 (1-800-242-8721)
www.americanheart.org

Centers for Disease Control and Prevention
1600 Clifton Road
Atlanta, GA 30333
Tel: 1-800-CDC-INFO (1-800-232-4636)
www.cdc.gov

IBS Self Help and Support Group
1440 Whalley Avenue, #145
New Haven, CT 06515
Tel: 203-404-0660
www.ibsgroup.org

National Institutes of Health
9000 Rockville Pike
Bethesda, MD 20892
Tel: 301-496-4000
www.nih.gov

The Food Allergy & Anaphylaxis Network
11781 Lee Jackson Hwy., Suite 160,
Fairfax, VA 22033-3309
Tel: 1-800-929-4040
faan@foodallergy.org
www.foodallergy.org

USDA Food and Nutrition Information Center
National Agricultural Library
10301 Baltimore Avenue, Room 105
Beltsville, MD 20705
Tel: 301-504-5414
www.nutrition.gov

U.S. Department of Health & Human Services
200 Independence Avenue, S.W.
Washington, D.C. 20201
Tel: 1-877-696-6775
www.healthfinder.gov

UNITED KINGDOM
Allergy UK
3 White Oak Square, London Road,
Swanley, Kent BR8 7A
Allergy Helpline: +44 (0)1322 619 898
info@allergyuk.org
www.allergyuk.org

The Anaphylaxis Campaign
PO Box 275, Farnborough GU14 6SX
Tel: +44 (0)1252 546 100
info@anaphylaxis.org.uk
www.anaphylaxis.org.uk

British Dietetic Association
5th Floor, Charles House, 148/9 Great
Charles Street, Queensway, Birmingham
B3 3HT
Tel: +44 (0)121 200 8080
info@bda.uk.com
www.bda.uk.com

The British Nutrition Foundation
High Holborn House, 52-54 High Holborn,
London WC1V 6RQ
Tel: +44 (0)20 7404 6504
postbox@nutrition.org.uk
www.nutrition.org.uk

Coeliac UK
Suites A-D Octagon Court, High Wycombe,
Bucks. HP11 2HY
Tel: +44 (0)1494 437 278
www.coeliac.co.uk

IRELAND
Irish Nutrition & Dietetic Institute
Ashgrove House, Kill Avenue, Dun Laoghaire,
Dean's Grange, County Dublin, Ireland
Tel: +353 (0)1280 4839
www.indi.ie

ITALY
Food Allergy Italia
Piazza De Gasperi, 45/a, Via Paolotti 7,
35131 Padova
Tel: +39 (0)34 0239 1230
info@foodallergy.it
www.foodallergyitalia.org

CANADA
Association Quebecoise des Allergies Alimentaires
5170 Dixie Road, Suite 204, Mississauga,
Ontario L4W 1E3
Tel: +1 (1)905 507 6208
www.aqaa.qc.ca

Dietitians of Canada
480 University Ave, Suite 604, Toronto,
Ontario M5G 1V2
Tel: +1 (1)416 596 0857
www.dietitians.ca

AUSTRALIA
Anaphylaxis Alliance
PO Box 3182, Asquith, NSW 2077
Tel: +61 (0)1300 728 000
www.allergyfacts.org.au

NEW ZEALAND
Allergy New Zealand
PO Box 56117, Dominion Road, Auckland
Tel: +64 (0)9623 3912
www.allergy.org.nz

SOUTH AFRICA
Allergy Society of South Africa
PO Box 88, Observatory, 7935
Cape Town, R.S.A.
Tel: +27 (0)21 447 9019
www.allergysa.org

Dairy-free Products

If you are unable to obtain dairy-free products at your local store or health food store, contact the manufacturers directly:

USA
Devansoy
206 West Seventh Street, PO Box 885,
Carroll, Iowa 51401
TEL: 1-712-792-9665
info@devansoy.com
www.devansoy.com
Soy milks and soy flours

Eat In The Raw
PO Box 682, Ashland, OR 97520
Tel: 541-665-0348
www.eatintheraw.com
Parma-vegan, parmesan alterna-cheese made using only raw organic walnuts, nutritional yeast, and Celtic sea salt

Tofutti US
50 Jackson Drive, Cranford, New Jersey 07016
Tel: 1-908-272-2400
Info@tofutti.com
www.tofutti.com
Dairy-free soy product specialists

UNITED KINGDOM & IRELAND
Alpro UK Ltd
Provamel
Altendiez Way, Latimer Business Park, Burton Latimer, Northants. NN15 5YT
Tel: +44 (0)1536 720 605
www.alprosoya.co.uk
Soy milk, yogurt, cream, dessert alternatives and rice milk alternative with calcium

Cauldron Foods
PO Box 181, Stokesley,
Middlesborough, TS9 7WU
Tel: +44 (0)845 602 1519
www.cauldronfoods.co.uk
Tofu specialists

Haldane Foods
Howard Way, Newport Pagnell,
Bucks. MK16 9PY
Tel: +44 (0)1908 211 311
info@haldanefoods.co.uk
Soy milk and meat alternatives

Plamil Foods
Folkestone, Kent CT19 6PQ
Tel: +44 (0)1303 850 588
contact-us@plamilfoods.co.uk
www.plamilfoods.co.uk
Soy milk, yogurt, cream, and dessert alternatives

The Redwood Wholefood Company
Redwood House, Burkitt Road, Earlstrees Industrial Estate, Corby, Northants NN17 4DT
Tel: +44 (0)1536 400 557
info@redwoodfoods.co.uk
www.redwoodfoods.co.uk
Dairy-free "cheezly" cheese range–super-melting cheddar, mozzarella, Edam and Gouda

AUSTRALIA
Sweet William Dairy-Free Chocolate
www.sweetwilliam.com.au

SOUTH AFRICA
South African Soyfood Association
info@soyfood.co.za
www.soyfood.co.za

index

dedication

This book is dedicated to all members of my family, especially my mother and my loving son, Timothy. Their eternal support, encouragement, and even criticism have been second to none. **Mini C**

For my wonderful Mum and Dad, Bill and Rita Carr, two of my greatest teachers and friends, with much love. **Tanya Haffner**

Acknowledgements
Mini C: Thanks to my mother, Surapee Mudita Karnasuta, who taught me to aim high but always to keep my feet on the ground. With her endless love and sacrifices I have come to realize that great achievements always come from within when you know in your heart that you have your loved ones all the way behind you. I would also like to give special thanks to my nanny, Sunee, who is in her mid-80s, and who was the first chef at my restaurant in London, for showing me the most traditional and complicated methods in Thai cooking. Without this awareness, I would not have been able to create and adapt recipes for today's hectic lifestyle that also have authentic tastes and textures. I would like to thank all my friends who gave me great advice and to the brave ones that made a real sacrifice to be my guinea pigs—you could say my recipes have been tried and tested! I would also like to thank God for giving me a chance to spend more than half of my life abroad. If not for this, I would not have had the chance to become familiar with Western and other foreign dishes, and learn to cook them the way I have!

Tanya Haffner: Thanks to my family, friends, and colleagues for all for their ongoing help and encouragement, and particular thanks to my fab sisters, Zoë and Heather—such blessings in my life. A very special thank you to my darling husband Shalom, for his encouragement, humor and love, and for Eli, our scrumptious phlegmatic son, born in the middle of writing this book. Lastly a big thank you to Jenny, Muna, Ana, and Ruth at Kyle Cathie—what a recipe for success—you are such pros and all so lovely with it!